Islam and the West

Conflict or Cooperation?

By the same author

The Rise and Fall of the Shah

The Afghanistan Conflict: Gorbachev's Options

The Soviet Withdrawal from Afghanistan (*with William Maley, co-editor*)

Refugees in the Modern World (*editor*)

Regime Change in Afghanistan: Foreign Intervention and the Politics of Legitimacy (*with William Maley*)

Russia in Search of its Future (*with William Maley, co-editor*)

The Middle East: Prospects for Peace and Stability? (*with Geoffrey Jukes, co-editor*)

Lebanon Beyond 2000 (*with Geoffrey Jukes, co-editor*)

Turkey: A Bridge between East and West (*editor*)

The Emerging Powers: The Cases of China, India, Iran, Iraq and Israel

Democratization in the Middle East: Experiences, Struggles, Challenges (*with Albrecht Schnabel, co-editor*)

Islam and the West
Conflict or Cooperation?

Amin Saikal

First published 2003 by
PALGRAVE MACMILLAN
Houndmills, Basingstoke, Hampshire RG21 6XS and
175 Fifth Avenue, New York, N.Y. 10010
Companies and representatives throughout the world

PALGRAVE MACMILLAN is the global academic imprint of the Palgrave
Macmillan division of St. Martin's Press, LLC and of Palgrave
Macmillan Ltd. Macmillan® is a registered trademark in the
United States, United Kingdom and other countries. Palgrave is a
registered trademark in the European Union and other countries.

ISBN 1–4039–0357–3 hardback
ISBN 1–4039–0358–1 paperback

This book is printed on paper suitable for recycling and made from fully
managed and sustained forest sources.

A catalogue record for this book is available from the British Library.

A catalog record for this book is available from the Library of Congress.

10 9 8 7 6 5 4 3 2 1
12 11 10 09 08 07 06 05 04 03

Printed and bound in Great Britain by
Creative Print & Design (Wales), Ebbw Vale

For Mary-Lou, Rahima, Samra and Amina – the delights of my life

Contents

Acknowledgements

This book, grounded in a long period of cumulative research, has been shaped by extensive intellectual discourse that I have had at both personal and academic levels with a number of valued friends and colleagues over the last few years. While being thankful to all of them, I must register my gratitude to six of them in particular.

First of all, my special thanks go to two long-standing friends and constant intellectual companions: William Maley and Greg Fry. Both in their individual and diverse ways have been tremendous sources of encouragement, support and critique. They have enriched me by not only reading the manuscript and providing me with much needed criticism, but also by their very warm friendship, lifting me up when I have felt pressured by this project and many more difficult ones during the long years of my academic life. I am deeply indebted to both of them. I must note that while Greg planted the idea of this book in me, it was William who kept me going to finish it.

The other person who read the manuscript and allowed me to benefit from his vast knowledge of history and critical memory is my former PhD supervisor and now an esteemed colleague and friend, Geoffrey Jukes. He has indeed been a gift to me and to dozens of other PhD scholars whom he has trained over a long period of a very successful academic life.

I am also grateful to Stuart Harris, who provided me with much criticism and challenged me vigorously to make sure that I took into account all the counter-arguments while writing the book. I have deeply appreciated his critical sharp mind and counsel.

I am equally indebted to my generous and thoughtful friend, Khalifa Bakhit Al-Falasi, whose enlightened perspective on the Middle East and loyalty to Islam, as well as his humanity, make him a great man.

Last but not least, I cannot say thank you enough to Carol Laslett, who never spared any effort to take on many of my administrative responsibilities to give me the time that I needed to invest in the research and writing of the book. She did so with a smile, patience and good humour. I extend thanks also to John Hart for commenting on parts of the manuscript, and to Leanne Harrison for locating some of the much needed research material.

Further, I am very thankful to Steven Kennedy of Palgrave Macmillan for his encouragement in the first place that I undertake this project, and for being a wonderfully supportive and patient editor.

Finally, this book would not have materialized had it not been for the support and love of Mary-Lou. She not only helped me with reading and formatting this book, but as always she tolerated me for what I am, and took on more family responsibilities than ever before so that I could focus on my writing. I just want simply to say: Mary-Lou, you are the best...

I must also thank the Australian National University for its support, and hundreds of my students who have challenged me year after year to remain true to the value of academic objectivity.

However, I take responsibility for the entire content of the book.

AMIN SAIKAL

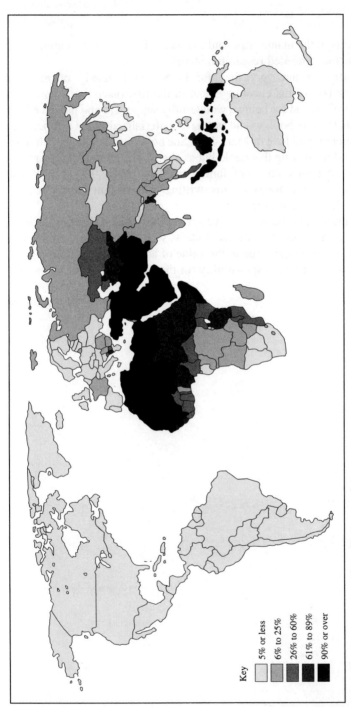

Muslim Population as Proportion of Total Population

Source: Data from islamicweb.com

Key

5% or less

6% to 25%

26% to 60%

61% to 89%

90% or over

Introduction

Relations between the 'West' and 'the domain of Islam' are now tense, to say the least. The September 11, 2001 events not only shook the USA and its allies, but also sent shockwaves through the Muslim world, sharply escalating differences that were already there. The relations are both complex and multidimensional, containing elements of conflict and cooperation, perception and misperception, and cultural and social differences. However, the tension has its roots more in political and politically motivated perceptual differences, its intensity fluctuating according to the political utility of the issues which have occasioned the two sides to expose their differences. In this context, the Western and Muslim entities are now more fearful and distrustful of one another than at any other time in contemporary history. A Western contention, which has resonated more strongly in Washington than in any other Western capital, sees those forces of political Islam which defy US control or influence as a serious threat to Western interests that must therefore be combated in whatever way necessary. Equally, a widespread fear exists among not only the radical and neofundamentalist political forces of Islam but also moderate Islamists and ordinary Muslims in general, that US 'Cold Warrior realists' have found it in their interest to exaggerate the notion of an 'Islamic threat' – to maintain a Western sense of superiority and hegemony over the Muslim world. They see the result as US promotion in the West of 'Islamophobia'.

It is interesting to note that this turmoil now dominates international politics even though Islamic radicalism was not a major issue in world affairs until the 1970s. Of all the Muslim states, many of which achieved independence after the Second World War, only one was subjected to theocratic rule – that is Saudi Arabia, with which the USA had already forged a very close partnership. Another Muslim state that was seeking to promote an Islamic national identity and unity, but had difficulty in making clear headway, was Pakistan. From its inception in 1947, that country was torn between a drive to have Islam as an overarching national factor, and a commitment to develop a Westminster system of democratic government, which essentially, for its success, required secularization of the state. The only time that Pakistan experienced an intense process of 're-Islamization' was during General Zia ul-Haq's military rule (1977–88), which the USA supported in the context of its opposition to the Soviet occupation of Afghanistan in the 1980s. Apart from Saudi Arabia and Pakistan, all other Muslim states, both old and new, were under the rule of either secularist or semi-secularist forces. This is not to deny that a variety of Islamist forces were at *work* in most of the Muslim domain, but these forces lacked the strength to challenge the dominance of their secular and semi-secular counterparts in both political and economic settings. The situation started unravelling in the 1970s, sliding rapidly towards the growth of political Islamism as an ideology of reform, opposition and resistance. In some countries political Islam succeeded in taking over the reins of power, as in the case of Iran and subsequently in the Sudan and post-communist Afghanistan, culminating in the rise to power of the extremist Taliban and the consolidation of Osama Bin Laden's Al Qaeda network.

In this work, 'the West' refers to those North American, West European and Australasian democracies that have evolved and functioned as a somewhat coherent political and military alliance, under US leadership since the Second World War (especially when faced by a common threat), despite differences arising from identity, cultural, social and political diversity within the alliance that have often led to divergent foreign policy interests and approaches. The 'domain of Islam' refers to all Arab and non-Arab followers of the religion of Islam, whether living in countries where Islam is the dominant religion or residing as minorities elsewhere. It signifies a common broad religious affiliation, without denying the existence among Muslims of multiple interpretations of Islam and national identities, based on diverse historical, sectarian, cultural, social and political differences, which since Islam's early centuries have rarely allowed Muslims to act in a unified fashion on the world stage. Nor does it imply the absence of rivalries and conflicts which have often marred relations among Muslim states in modern times.

This book's central objective is to examine the nature of the growing tension between the West and the domain of Islam by seeking to answer three fundamental questions. What has gone wrong in both historical and contemporary terms? To what extent do Muslims bear responsibility and in what ways has Western, and more specifically

US, policy behaviour contributed to diluting the relations between the two sides? What is the way forward to repair the damage by building the necessary bridges of understanding and promoting a more peaceful coexistence between the two entities, as an important foundation for generating a lasting, stable and equitable world order? To this end, the book focuses on three major topics: first, the features that have united or divided the Western and Muslim worlds in the course of history, allowing them to enjoy durable periods of peaceful coexistence on the one hand, and stints of misunderstanding and conflict on the other; second, the great issues that have sharpened tension and reduced the chances of harmony in their relations in recent times; and third, the issues whose viable resolution could overcome some of the major obstacles in improving their relations in a globalized world. In addressing these questions, the book builds on and ranges beyond the excellent analyses in monographs such as John L. Esposito's *Unholy War: Terror in the Name of Islam*, and Giles Kepel's *Jihad: The Trail of Political Islam*.

Of course, the multidimensionality of relations between Muslim and Western states has given rise to spheres of interaction in which religion, either as a value system or as a marker of communal difference, is a peripheral factor. Commercial relations provide a case in point. While the USA, for example, has put in place legal constraints on certain kinds of economic relations with Iran, many other Western states have been prepared to exploit entrepreneurial opportunities which they see as arising. Iranian graduate students study at European and Australian universities, many Western countries have 'normal' diplomatic relations with Iran, and the Middle Eastern state that is subject to the most stringent international sanctions – Iraq – has been targeted not because of anything to do with religion, but rather on account of its August 1990 violation (through its invasion of Kuwait) of a constitutive element of the Westphalian international system, as well as specific prohibitions in the UN Charter.

This book does not provide an overview of all aspects of relations between Western states and states in which Muslims are a numerical majority of the population. Rather, it is concerned with ways in which interpretations or perceptions of the religion of Islam and of the character and behaviour of the West can and have complicated relations between the West and those states. Semi-secular forces in the Muslim world are far from trivial; indeed, many rulers in Muslim countries regard religion as either a personal matter, or a basis for legitimation of state power through subordinated 'official' religious establishments. However, these numerically significant semi-secularists, because of the very nature of their elite location, have proved less effective than their Islamist opponents in articulating values around which aggrieved forces can coalesce. The dilemma for semi-secularists is that they attract blame for what goes wrong, but little credit for what goes well, given that often they have no claim to 'democratic' legitimacy.

The book is divided into six chapters. Chapter 1 provides an overview of the events of September 11 and their aftermath, with an exposé of various views of Islam and Muslims expressed in the West, and the different attitudes which have coalesced among Muslims towards the West, especially the USA. The purpose is to provide a setting rather than to detail the September 11 events and those that transpired after them, which in many ways are still unfolding.

Chapter 2 explores the shared religious values of Islam, Christianity and Judaism, and examines the ways in which harmonious relations evolved and were maintained, and differences and conflicts were managed among these three great revealed religions. The idea is not to delve deep in history, but to tease out those issues which are relevant to understanding the background to what has transpired as major points of conflict between the two sides in modern times.

Chapter 3 looks at the rise of the USA to global power and the expansion of its interests in, and policy approach to, the Muslim domain. In particular, it assesses the US role in the context of US–Soviet Cold War rivalry and the USA's policy of containment of the Soviet Union, the ways a number of Muslim countries fell into the US orbit, and the ways the USA sought either to marginalize or to ignore a few Muslim nationalist challenges. It also explores Muslim perceptions of the US role.

Chapter 4 focuses on the major issues of tension and the USA's responses to them, which have sharply influenced Western–Muslim relations in recent times. I propose to examine the Iranian revolution of 1978–79, the Afghanistan conflict from the successful pro-Soviet coup of April 1978 to the fall of the Taliban in November 2001, and the Israeli–Arab conflict. With respect to the latter, the aim is to explain the impact of Israel's occupation of the Palestinian lands and the USA's support of Israel in enabling radical Islam to enter the Palestinian nationalist movement and to galvanize the political forces of Islam across the Muslim domain. I also evaluate the USA's handling of each issue in order to determine how much the USA's own conduct may have contributed to generating Muslim distrust or hostility. The chapter is designed not to give detailed coverage of these issues, which has been ably achieved by many other works, but to distil those components which have proved relevant to the tension in US relations with the Muslim domain.

Chapter 5 investigates the tension between the West and the domain of Islam in the context of a lack of democracy in most Muslim countries, in an attempt to see how much this factor has contributed to a sense of a dichotomy between state and society, and therefore alienation of ordinary citizens from their ruling elites and governments in Muslim countries. Some have argued that many problems of the Muslim domain have domestic roots, and that as long as this remains the case no amount of effort by outsiders to reach out to Muslims can generate solid understanding with them.

Chapter 6 investigates ways to move out of the current frame of hostility and mistrust into which the USA and its allies on one side and the Muslim peoples on the other are locked.

An extensive bibliography is provided for those who wish to follow up the issues raised in this book in more depth.

1
September 11 and its Aftermath

The apocalyptic attacks of September 11, 2001 on the World Trade Center in New York and the Pentagon in Washington, perpetrated by operatives of the wealthy Saudi dissident Osama Bin Laden and his extremist Islamic Al Qaeda (the Base) network, proved as multi-dimensional in their impact as relations have historically been between the multifaceted entities called 'the West', now led by the USA, and 'the domain of Islam'. The attacks were hugely destructive of lives, property and economic opportunities, profoundly symbolic in targeting the heart of the USA's global economic and political-military power, and potent in shattering the psyche of invulnerability of the USA and many of its allies around the world. They exposed US vulnerability to attacks and changed the USA's perceptions both of itself as the world's only secure superpower, and of the international order it had cherished since the end of the Cold War and collapse of the Soviet Union. In the past, the USA focused much of its intellectual and physical energy on a capacity to defend and assert itself against aggression by another state actor. The attacks struck at this paradigm of security. The enemy was no longer a state, but a sub-national actor with an extensive, shadowy international network, committed to what have been dubbed 'Armageddon-type' missions. The USA was now confronted with 'international terrorism' – violence waged to inflict maximum pain and suffering on a civilian population in pursuit of either specific or notional political objectives. It confronted the Republican Administration of President George W. Bush with new challenges, and made it recast its approach to the world and sub-stitute many old assumptions and policies with new ones in order to reassert the USA's superpower standing. It prompted the Administration to move rapidly to identify its enemy, and to set about creating a domestic and international environment to fight this enemy on all fronts.

However, what transpired has defocused US foreign policy, enmity has emerged on multiple fronts, many of the USA's allies are confused, and the world is left in a state of suspense. While the USA and many of its allies continue to fear the threat of when and how terrorism will hit them again, the followers of the Islamic faith have been widely offended, and have felt besieged by the USA's attempts to alleviate this fear. Washington's resort to military might, without a well-crafted, coherent political strategy, has sharpened hostility and distrust between the West and the domain of Islam.

The September 11 attacks challenged the USA and changed the terms of reference for it on many issues in numerous ways. They exposed a colossal failure by US intelligence agencies, especially the CIA and FBI. Their inability to avert the attacks led to a Congressional Inquiry into their efficiency and to an overhaul of their role and operations, with a Presidential proposal to create a new super-Department of Homeland Security,[1] to retool the USA's protective services. They highlighted the weaknesses in US military preparedness in dealing with non-state actors, prompting President Bush to propose the highest military expenditure in 20 years to develop new high-technology weapons and methods of operation especially designed to fight terrorism. By June 2002, the Bush Administration expediently embraced a new strategic doctrine to enable the USA to bomb first and explain later. The doctrine exalted the primacy of preemptive strikes against terrorists and hostile countries possessing chemical, biological or nuclear weapons, and essentially sidelined containment and deterrence, the two key pillars of US behaviour during the Cold War.[2]

Beyond this, the terrorist attacks shattered the USA's sense of immunity from the way that globalization – the phenomenon of large-scale interdependence, which has come to dominate the world deeper and faster than at any other time in history, especially in the areas of mass communications, capital, and technology transfer – could be used by hostile forces to damage the USA itself. With its control of information technology and expansive corporate influence, the USA had grown very comfortable as the main beneficiary of the phenomenon. It had been prepared to overlook many of its predatory aspects,[3] to which many poor countries had been subjected, in order to safeguard and strengthen its own interests as the determinant of the well-being of the world as a whole. It was the terrorists' relatively cheap but effective use of transcontinental means of communications, finance and technological innovations that enabled them to target some of the landmarks that symbolized the US position as the most powerful state on earth. Washington was also alerted to the danger that determined, hostile sub-national actors, supported by certain state actors, might now go even further to obtain and use weapons of mass destruction as easily as they had attacked the World Trade Center and the Pentagon. Washington now had to look seriously at the issue of 'globalization vulnerability', and examine its own role in it. This has led it to impose stringent controls on people movement, financial and technological transfers, and foreigners' use of US facilities and know-how at home and abroad. In other words, the USA has engaged in activities that are in many ways anti-globalization in character – a development which could have serious ramifications for the shape of the world order in coming years.

Until September 11, the USA and most of its allies shared a general assumption that poverty, lack of education and social deprivation generated violence and terrorism. The President of the World Bank, Paul Wolfensohn, regularly stressed the importance of this relationship, calling for rich countries to help poor countries and to create an international environment conducive to the generation of long term structural peace and stability. Yet less attention was given to the possibility that a combination of religious extremism, wealth, and political causes in the context of a globalized world could prove more deadly than poverty and social deprivation in producing unprecedented terrorist violence. The September 11 events changed this, at least for the USA and many of its Western allies. Bin Laden and his followers, most importantly the hijackers who flew the planes into the World Trade Center and Pentagon, typically came from very wealthy and well educated, but disaffected, Arab backgrounds, with 15 of the 19 hijackers coming from one of the USA's key Arab Islamic allies, Saudi Arabia. Thus, they acted neither out of poverty, nor in pursuit of wealth.

This shifted the debate in the USA in favour of Samuel Huntington's prediction of the coming age as one of conflicts between various cultures and civilizations, with the West and Islam as main protagonists. He states: 'Conflicts between the West and Islam … focus less on territory than on broader intercivilizational issues such as weapons proliferation, human rights and democracy, control of oil, migration, Islamist terrorism, and Western interven-tion'.[4] He calls on Western policy makers to ensure that the West gets stronger and fends off all the others, Islam in particular. He is, of course, widely criticized for relying on a vague notion of what he calls 'civilizational identity', adopting a tautological approach to define Western and Islamic civilizations as somewhat homogeneous and self-contained. Edward Said criticizes him for having little

> time to spare for the internal dynamics and plurality of every civil-isation, or for the fact that the major contest in most modern cultures concerns the definition or interpretation of each culture, or for the unattractive possibility that a great deal of demagogy and ignorance is involved in presuming to speak for a whole religion or civilisation. No, the West is the West and Islam Islam.[5]

Despite these criticisms, Huntington has claimed that the September 11 attacks vindicate his thesis, especially since the attack-ers acted for causes which did not emanate from poverty. This line of thinking now seems to have gained increasing legitimacy in Washington's corridors of power. However, it needs to be treated with a good deal of caution. The causes which drive alienated forces into the arms of a terrorist such as Bin Laden are strongly political in character, and emanate from specific historical circumstances rather than from broad 'civilizational' identity. Nor do the reactions of forces within the Muslim world to the September 11 attacks point to a homogeneity of the type that Huntington's analysis implies. For example, when Kabul was liberated from the Taliban on November 13, 2001, Western journalists reported scenes of wild celebration in the streets of the Afghan capital. Such episodes should give pause to those who see Western values as threatened by an undifferenti-ated 'Islam'. Many devout Muslims have no particular desire to live under the yoke of a religious autocracy, and many Afghans have indi-cated that they are prepared to accept a prolonged Western presence in their country to thwart externally imposed religious extremism, as long as it does not degenerate into an imposition of cultural hegemony.

Confronted with the September 11 outrages, the Bush Administration scrambled for an appropriate response strategy to achieve a number of short and long term objectives. The immediate aims understandably were to soothe public anger and despair, and restore Americans' confidence in themselves and in their country's power; to send a decisive signal to hostile forces everywhere that the USA would not be pushed around; and to reassert its superpower status at home and abroad. The distant objectives focused on shaping a world environment which would tighten the noose as much as possible around anti-US elements, but widen the opportunities for the USA to safeguard and entrench its interests, way of life and modus operandi against anti-status quo developments.

The first set of objectives led President Bush, who had assumed power in January 2001 with an avowed policy goal of enhancing US global power without becoming overly preoccupied with foreign policy, to adopt a two-pronged political and military response. He denounced the prime suspect, Bin Laden and his Al Qaeda network, as terrorists, devoid of any claim to morality, virtue or reason, and proclaimed the USA and its allies the repository of morality, freedom, justice, democracy and civilization. Thus, by definition, Bin Laden, his network, and those supporting them were delegitimized. Within this frame, the USA set out to build an international coalition to launch military, diplomatic and economic campaigns against global terrorism, punish the perpetrators of the attacks on the USA, and destroy their most visible sanctuaries and infrastructures as swiftly as possible. The Bush Administration also announced that the campaign would probably take months and years, since the Al Qaeda network was comprehensive, with cells in some 60 countries. Although the axe must immediately fall on Afghanistan, where Bin Laden and his key lieutenants were based, protected by the ruling medievalist Islamic Taliban militia, Washington made it clear that its campaign could involve additional targets in the Muslim domain and beyond.

As American patriotism surged, and international moral legitimacy and sympathy for the USA gathered pace, the Bush Administration was able to move with unprecedented impunity to achieve its objectives. A mindset took shape very much reminiscent of the Cold War in the 1950s. It divided the world's state actors into good and evil, giving them only two choices: 'you are either with us or against us'.[6] Just as in the 1950s and part of the 1960s where the USA made no distinction between different types of communism, treating the Soviet, Chinese and Vietnamese variants as the same, and opposed some Third World nationalism and neutralism as aligned with communism, the Bush Administration now adopted a blanket definition of international terrorism. It postulated that all hostile acts by sub-national actors and supported by states, irrespective of their causes and objectives, were in principle condemnable and punishable, drawing no distinction between mindless acts of violence perpetrated on a civilian population, and acts by states and subjugated peoples in the name of self-defence or resistance.

It set out to treat, for example, Al Qaeda's attacks on the USA, and Palestinian acts of despair, involving suicide bombings, as equally morally repugnant, and politically unacceptable, even though the latter owed much to Israel's repressive occupation of Palestinian territories and application of disproportionate force to maintain its occupation. This was despite the fact that in the 1980s, a number of US political figures and most US allies had supported the actions of the African National Congress, including assassination and bombing of civilians, as part of legitimate resistance to the apartheid regime in South Africa. It took no notice of the view that, as Zbigniew Brzezinski writes,

American involvement in the Middle East is clearly the main impulse of the hatred that has been directed at America. There is no escaping the fact that Arab political emotions have been shaped by the region's encounter with French and British colonialism, by the defeat of the Arab effort to prevent the existence of Israel and by the subsequent American support for Israel and its treatment of the Palestinians, as well as by the direct injection of American power into the region.[7]

Nor did it pay any attention to the belief subsequently expressed by most Europeans in a survey, conducted by the German Marshall Fund of the United States in conjunction with the Chicago Council on Foreign Relations, that US foreign policy contributed to the events of September 11.[8]

The USA also decided to take no account of whether a regime was democratic or dictatorial and respected or violated human rights, as long as it was prepared to side with the USA in its hour of need. Washington held out the promise of substantial rewards for those states that shared its approach, and of isolation and castigation for those that failed to come aboard. The approach was initially successful, as no state wanted to be identified with international terrorism. It enabled the USA to build a broad coalition, including not only all its European allies, Japan, Australia and New Zealand, but also a number of key Muslim states – most importantly Pakistan (hitherto the main sponsor of the Taliban and the latter's alliance with Al Qaeda), Egypt, all the Gulf Arab states, and Indonesia, Russia, China and India. Even the USA's traditional enemy, the Islamic Republic of Iran, acquiesced to its request for cooperation.

Within a month of September 11, the USA was able to launch 'Operation Enduring Freedom', a military campaign to destroy Bin Laden and Al Qaeda as well as the Taliban regime. Despite its earlier-expressed opposition to involvement in the difficult and messy task of nation-building, it found itself with little choice but to do precisely that. By December 2001, US forces had bombed the Taliban and Al Qaeda out of power. They were assisted in the ground fighting by the Afghan anti-Taliban forces, the United Front, motivated more powerfully than ever by Al Qaeda agents' assassination of their charismatic and legendary leader, Commander Ahmed Shah Massoud, on September 9. This opened the way for a more internationally acceptable government to be formed in Afghanistan. Under UN auspices but US influence, the United Front negotiated a power-sharing arrangement with a group associated with former Afghan King Mohammed Zahir Shah, who had been living in exile in Rome since his overthrow in 1973, and two other mainly exile-based groups that represented a tribal mixture of ethnic Pashtuns, traditionally the largest ethnic group in Afghanistan, and to which most of the Taliban belonged.

The result was the setting up of a broad-based Interim Government under a previously little known, but moderate and modernist pro-American Pashtun figure, Hamid Karzai. This government was to last six months, its main function being to hold a traditional Afghan Grand Council (Loya Jirga) to create a transitional government for another two years, after which elections would be held. The USA and the Karzai government declared a lasting partnership, and the USA and the international community as a whole pledged to rebuild Afghanistan and never to allow it to become a nest for international terrorism. Although the USA and its allies could not capture Bin Laden, the Taliban leader Mullah Mohammed Omar or most of their top lieutenants, they scored a number of important successes. They changed the regime in Afghanistan, opening a rare opportunity for a settlement of the conflict after 23 years of warfare and two invasions – one overtly by the Soviet Union and another covertly by Pakistan through the Taliban and Al Qaeda. They also enticed Pakistan's military ruler, General Pervez Musharraf, to cooperate fully with the

USA against Pakistan's clients, and enlisted the support of the Central Asian governments, especially those of Uzbekistan and Tajikistan, which border Afghanistan, for their Afghan campaign. As its forces secured operational bases in Afghanistan and these countries, the USA achieved a position of preeminence in the region unprecedented since its loss of Iran to the anti-American Islamic revolutionary regime of Ayatollah Khomeini in 1979.

The USA was very careful to portray its campaign as directed against terrorism and barbarism, not Islam and Muslims *per se*. Washington's main message was that Islam had been hijacked by a group of terrorists, whose actions could find no justification in Islam. To soothe Muslim discontent, British Prime Minister Tony Blair made it his task, in a series of eloquent and well crafted speeches in October–December 2001, to reinforce Bush's messages that the West had high respect for Islam as a religion of peace and tolerance, and had no quarrels with either Islam or Muslims, but only with those who had demeaned Islam by invoking its name to justify evil and barbaric acts. He engaged in a flurry of diplomatic visits and activities to calm anger across the Muslim world over the USA's war in Afghanistan, and to impress upon the world that the USA and its allies were concerned with justice and consistency, and therefore held no grudge against Arabs, Islam or its adherents because Bin Laden and his followers had committed despicable acts of terrorism in Islam's name.

For a moment, it even appeared that both Washington and London had decided the time had come to remove a major anomaly in the USA's Middle East policy: the existence of one standard for its strategic partner, Israel, and another for Arabs. They went on a diplomatic offensive to display unprecedentedly firm commitment to securing a resolution of the Palestinian problem, based on the creation of a viable independent Palestinian state. In a rare display of moral equivalence between the plight of the Afghan and Palestinian peoples, Prime Minister Blair acknowledged Western mistakes in abandoning the Afghan people in the past, thus allowing their country to become a source of international terrorism, and possibly not doing enough to resolve the Palestinian problem, which is a source of growing anti-American and for that matter anti-Western sentiment among Muslims in general, and Arabs in particular. While affirming the need to remain engaged in Afghanistan and rebuild the country on a long term basis, he intimated that failure to resolve the Palestinian problem had provided fertile ground for recruitment for Bin Laden and his like. In a policy statement in March 2002, US Secretary of State Colin Powell for the first time even endorsed the notion of an independent Palestinian state; the United Nations Security Council took this up in its Resolution 1397 (March 12, 2002) by affirming 'a vision of a region where two States, Israel and Palestine, live side by side within secure and recognised borders'.[9] As violence spiralled and Israel in April 2002 made its biggest military incursions into the Palestinian territories since its relinquishment of control of most of them to the newly created Palestinian Authority (PA), led by Yasser Arafat, under the Oslo Peace accords of 1993, the USA promised more active mediation to resolve the Palestinian problem.

Meanwhile, London and Washington hastened to do everything possible to shore up General Musharraf's position against numerous radical Pakistani Islamic groups supporting Bin Laden and the Taliban. Of course, many of these groups had previously been supported to varying degrees by Pakistan's military intelligence (ISI) to assist in ensuring Pakistan's domination of Afghanistan through Taliban and Al Qaeda rule, and Pakistan's backing of Islamic militants fighting India's rule of predominantly Muslim Jammu and Kashmir. But now Washington and its allies deemed it expedient to embrace General Musharraf as a frontline partner against terror and reward him not only politically, financially and economically, but also by forgiving him and his military and intelligence machines for demolishing democracy in Pakistan and for what had transpired under the Taliban–Al Qaeda rule in Afghanistan.

None of these policy steps, however, could hide the multiplicity of views that concurrently emerged in the West about Islam and Muslims, and the diverse concerns and distrust that intensified in the Muslim world about US motives and objectives after September 11. The views emanating from the USA in particular, and its European and Australian allies in general, were on the whole of three kinds.

The first was contained in official statements that by and large emphasized the non-religious, non-ethnic and non-racist character of the campaign against terror, insisting that it was directed only against those who had used and abused Islam for their own misguided selfish, messianic ends. The only important slippage in this respect came early on from President Bush when he described the war as a 'crusade'. This term reminded Muslims of the medieval Christian crusades, which resulted in much brutality against the Muslim Arabs in Jerusalem, and immediately drew widespread criticism that forced the White House to withdraw the term.

The second was embodied in Italian Prime Minister Silvio Berlusconi's description of Western civilization as superior to that of Islam, as 'it has guaranteed well-being, respect for human rights and – in contrast with Islamic countries – respect for religious and political rights'. Berlusconi also hoped 'the West will continue to conquer [Muslim] peoples, like it conquered communism'.[10] Although he retracted this view under international pressure, he was not the only one to express it. Many other opinion makers and commentators echoed such remarks in Western media in one form or another. For example, the US Attorney General, John Ashcroft, reportedly stated: 'Islam is a religion in which God requires you to send your son to die. Christianity is a faith in which God sends his son to die for you.'[11]

The third view directly denounced Islam as a religion that inspired terrorism and produced terrorists. Several US congressmen and leading Western commentators launched a campaign to vilify Islam and condemn oil rich Saudi Arabia, for having promoted the kind of Islam, nurtured the kind of education at home, and supported the kind of activities abroad, including religious schools or *madrasas* in Pakistan and elsewhere in the Muslim domain, that produced Al Qaeda, many of its operatives, and most of the Taliban fighters in Afghanistan. They questioned the value of the USA's close ties with Saudi Arabia, based primarily on the principle of the USA providing security to the theocratic Saudi regime in return for its ensuring a ready supply of oil to the West and providing the USA with important strategic bases for maintaining US dominance in the region.[12]

The USA, and to varying degrees its allies, accompanied expressions of such views with a series of tough policy and security measures that by and large singled out Muslims, particularly those from Arab backgrounds, for discriminatory investigation and treatment. Hundreds – many of them US citizens – were detained without trial in the USA, which also instituted severe procedures to monitor immigrants and visitors from the Arab/Muslim world. While in some cases these measures have been rewarded by tracking down a number of Al Qaeda activists in the USA and Europe and possibly preventing more terrorist attacks, in many other cases they have resulted in distressing human rights violations contrary to all the principles for which the liberal democracies publicly stand. The US authorities have even sought to invoke a law adopted at the height of the 1950s McCarthyist witch-hunt for communists, to hunt down undesirable Arab/Muslim elements. They have also shut down the websites of many Muslim organizations, irrespective of their religious or political standing, depriving the Muslims of the educational means and freedoms cherished so dearly in the West.

Reactions to these developments in the domain of Islam have naturally been diverse and at various levels, proportionate to the pluralism that exists in the domain. At official levels, all governments, except that of the Iraqi ruler Saddam Hussein, condemned terrorism and supported, or acquiesced in, US moral authority and power to wage war against terror. Saddam Hussein's regime, given the venomous state of its relations with the USA, spitefully blamed US policy behaviour for the September 11 attacks. The only other regime that placed a caveat on its stand was the Islamic Republic of Iran; it had all along opposed the Taliban, but now also cautioned the USA over its military involvement in Afghanistan, though without any move to create obstacles. All other governments, including one of the USA's strongest critics, Libya, denounced those misusing Islam to justify killing innocent people, and branded such acts as contrary to the teachings of Islam. Many Muslims, after all, died trapped in the wreckage of the World Trade Center. The key Muslim countries – from Egypt and Saudi Arabia to Jordan, Pakistan, Malaysia and Indonesia – lined up behind the USA, although expressing the conviction that the USA must do everything possible to avoid civilian casualties in Afghanistan. Despite his growing frustration over the USA's consistent support of Israel, Palestinian Authority Chairman Arafat also expressed full sympathy for the USA, and made a public display of donating blood for the victims of the September 11 attacks.

However, this tells only one side of the story. Given the authoritarian nature of regimes in the Muslim countries (with the exception to varying extents of Iran, Indonesia, Turkey and Bangladesh) what governments said or did bore little relevance to how different segments of their populations felt and wanted to react. In Pakistan, radical supporters of Bin Laden and the Taliban created the impression that Pakistan could possibly explode, although they were numerically weak and Musharraf's military rule could easily contain them. Some Palestinians expressed happiness over the terrorist attacks as part of the resistance to the USA's support of Israel, and Egyptian and

Indonesian Islamic radicals staged sporadic demonstrations. On the whole, Washington felt confident that governments in other key Muslim states would control their populations, through being in various degrees either authoritarian allies of the USA, as in the case of Egypt, Jordan, Morocco, and the Arab states of the Gulf Cooperation Council, led by Saudi Arabia, or sufficiently dictatorial or authoritarian to disallow dissent, as in Iraq, Syria, Tunisia, Libya and Malaysia. To keep public outbursts in check, the Saudi authorities reportedly arrested several thousand radical Islamists. The United Arab Emirates and several other Arab countries acted similarly, though on a smaller scale. In addition, unconfirmed reports claimed that some two hundred military officers in Egypt and dozens in Jordan, who wanted to challenge their governments, were imprisoned.

This indicated little about the fact that public emotions below government levels were, and still are, running high in the domain of Islam. In a Gallup Poll survey of public opinion carried out in the weeks following September 11 in nine key Muslim countries, while 67 per cent of respondents described the September 11 events as morally unjustifiable, a majority of them also registered deep grievances against the West in general, and the USA in particular. They in a way identified with Bin Laden's cause by stressing that they did not think that 'the United States and the nations of the West have respect for Arabs or for Islamic culture or religion', and that the West pays little attention to their situation and 'makes few attempts to communicate or to create cross-cultural bridges'. Fifty-three per cent maintained an unfavourable view of the USA, and 58 per cent expressed dislike for President George W. Bush.[13]

Citizens all over the Muslim world found themselves squeezed to suffocation in one way or another between domestic repression and external vilification. They felt anger over the way they had been forced to defend their religion and Islamic identity, and despaired over the way the USA and its allies were claiming moral virtue irrespective of their own often contradictory behaviour towards Muslims. While disapproving of what had happened on September 11, and while maintaining that Islam was a religion of peace, tolerance and forgiveness, many could not understand how the USA and its allies could simply dismiss Bin Laden and his operatives as terrorists, without asking the main question: why did they do it? From their perspectives, neither Bin Laden nor his operatives were uneducated lunatics, and they acted not in a vacuum but in the context of historical and contemporary causes that had motivated many Muslims to distrust and even resent the US government and some of its allies. They have remained frustrated that the question of *why* has found no meaningful space in the debate about September 11 in the West, and in particular in the USA.

If they were pleased by earlier US and British pronouncements regarding the urgent need to resolve the Palestinian problem, they rapidly found their optimism misplaced. Once the USA and its allies had Bin Laden, his Al Qaeda activists and their Taliban harbourers on the run, Washington's urgency about the Palestinian issues waned as quickly as it had waxed. President Bush shocked the Palestinians and their Arab and Muslim supporters when he decided to give a free hand to right-wing Israeli Prime Minister Ariel Sharon to exploit the legitimacy of the USA's war against terror to besiege Yasser Arafat in his headquarters, intensify Israel's suppression of Palestinian resistance, and subsequently seek to marginalize Arafat and effectively to put on hold the creation of an independent Palestinian state until such time as the Palestinians had a leadership palatable to Israel. Sharon is widely viewed among the Arabs and Muslims as a man not of peace but of war. His record of public service over the last 50 years has consistently testified to his dedication to the threefold goal of creating a 'Greater Israel', suppressing the Palestinians and humiliating the Arabs. President Bush's courting of him as 'a man of peace' and partner in war against terrorism caused outrage not just among the Palestinians, but across the domain of Islam. With Sharon applying maximum force to quell the second Palestinian *intifada* (uprising) which had begun in late 2000, involving tit-for-tat Palestinian suicide bombings and Israeli targeted assassination of Palestinian figures and massive retaliations, the television images night after night of unarmed and defenceless Palestinians killed and their properties either blown up or confiscated, while the Israeli settlements continued to expand, could only prove very disturbing to Muslims around the world.

Many among Arab and non-Arab Muslims, whose organic links and religious affinity with Palestinians and deep attachment to Jerusalem as Islam's third holiest site after Mecca and Medina cannot be underestimated, could see that the Bush Administration had blatantly sided with the occupier rather than the occupied, and the villain rather than the victim. They grew more than ever distrustful of the USA and those of its allies that gave it unqualified support.

Bearing in mind that, despite Islam's unity at doctrinal level, various interpretative Islams have historically come to prevail in the diverse Muslim world, four different attitudes have emerged to play a central part in reactions and debate in the Muslim domain about September 11 and its aftermath.

The first comes from those moderate Islamists who uphold Islam as a dynamic ideology of political and social transformation, and a meaningful ideology of opposition to authoritarian regimes at home, but reject any form of violence as a means of achieving such objectives, unless their religion, life and liberty either at individual or societal level are seriously threatened or invaded. Although they come in various forms, on the whole they subscribe to what has been termed 'Islamic liberalism' and adhere strictly to the Islamic command, as enshrined in the Qur'an, that there is no compulsion in religion. They operate mainly within loose organizations, informal small groups or at individual levels. They include the Iranian Islamic reformists, led by President Mohammed Khatami, the Indonesian Nahdatul Ulama (Awakening of Ulama) organization (now partly incorporated into a new political party, called Partai Kebangkit or National Awakening Party), headed by former Indonesian President Abdurrahman Wahid, and the now defunct Refah Partisi (Welfare Party) in Turkey, led by Necmettin Erbakan in the 1990s. Most Muslim intellectuals and informed Muslims fall into this category. They reject the September 11 attacks as unacceptable, and are pained to learn that Osama Bin Laden and his Al Qaeda were responsible for them. They have dissociated Islam from extremism and are appalled by those who have presumed to act in its name to take innocent lives, whether at home or abroad, and thereby place Muslims everywhere under siege in one form or another. They reject these people's extremist impositions on the Muslims over whom they have managed to gain control, such as the people of Afghanistan during Taliban rule. More importantly, they regard the September 11 events as providing a dangerous incentive to the USA and its allies to assume the higher moral ground to expand and deepen US dominance in the Muslim world, and marginalize defiant political Islam more than ever before.

They contend that no matter what their cause, Bin Laden and his operatives have managed, just as the secularist Saddam Hussein did by his foolish invasion of Kuwait in 1990, to set back by decades Muslim efforts to achieve domestic reform, independence from foreign interference and a possible strong voice in the international arena. They stress the value of peaceful, evolutionary change and want to work within existing national and international structures to bring about structural change. They are open to modernity, believe in the inevitability of progress, are well disposed to interfaith dialogue, and have no aversion to utilizing Western knowledge and achievements to benefit their societies within a globalized world.

Yet they simultaneously criticize the USA and some of its allies for not making the necessary efforts to develop better understanding of Muslim faith, norms, values and practices, to build solid bridges of understanding for mutually rather than unilaterally beneficial relationships. They reserve their harshest criticism for those US policy actions that either overlook the plight of the Palestinian people or highlight the behaviour of some extremist Islamic groups when convenient to tarnish the image of Muslims in general. Their attitude towards the USA and Western allies is one of love and dislike: keen to benefit from Western education and technology, and to secure access to Western countries as both migrants and visitors, but critical of Western policy behaviour towards the Muslim world and of arrogant claims of supremacy over Muslims. In Islamic terms, the moderate Islamists are on the whole *ijtihadi* – creatively interpretive of Islam, with dedication to renewal and reform as the best means to achieve salvation and prosperity.

The second attitude emanates from radical Islamists, who are again diverse in their ideological disposition and modus operandi, and share some of the platform of their moderate counterparts, especially in adherence to the fundamentals of Islam. However, they differ from the moderates in their puritanical disposition and orthodox political and social modus operandi. They want Sharia (Islamic Law) instituted as the foundation for operation of the state. They view political and social imposition and use of violence under certain circumstances as legitimate means to protect and assert their religion and religious-cultural identity, and to create the kind of polity they deem Islamic. They are not necessarily against modernity; but want to ensure that modernity and all its manifestations are adopted in conformity with their religious values and practices. They are prone to act radically to redress perceived historical and contemporary injustices inflicted upon Muslims by outsiders, but do not necessarily extend this to cover similar injustices committed by Muslim against Muslim.

At this juncture they challenge outside powers and their own governments for either being under the influence and control of those powers, or failing to respond effectively to domestic and foreign policy problems facing the Muslim domain. They hold the West, the USA in particular, responsible for the political, social, and economic plight and cultural decay of Muslims everywhere, and for the damage that European colonization and post-1945 American domination of most of the Muslim domain inflicted upon Muslims. They have often functioned more successfully in opposition than in power. Many groups in the Muslim world are of this nature. They range from some of the conservative (or what have become popularly known as hardline) followers of the leader of the Iranian revolution of 1978–79, Ayatollah Khomeini, who have achieved much greater power in Iran than their popular strength would ever allow, to Egypt's Ikhwan al-Muslimun (Muslim Brotherhood), especially under its charismatic leader, Sayyed Qutb, killed in prison in 1966, to the Sudanese National Islamic Front, led by Hassan Abdullah al-Turabi. Notwithstanding their apocalyptic, extremist activities, Bin Laden and many in his Al Qaeda leadership, as well as the Palestinian Hamas and Lebanese Hezbullah (which emerged more in response to Israeli occupation than anything else) also fall into this category. They characterize violent Muslim actions against the USA and its allies as legitimate responses to US behaviour.

They view the USA as their most dangerous enemy, not only for backing Israel's occupation of Palestinian lands, most importantly East Jerusaem, but also for propping up corrupt and dictatorial regimes in many Muslim countries, which they maintain the USA does in order to keep the Muslim world backward and to ensure US hegemonic dominance in world politics. They consider much of what has become an international crisis since September 11 to be a deliberate strategy of hard core realists of the Cold War era and 'reborn' Christians, who now dominate the Bush Administration, and who want to replace the Soviet Union with Islam as the enemy. Their views are often marked by intense hostility to the Jews. Many among them regard the USA and the civilization for which it stands as demeaning and repugnant to Islam and the Islamic way of life. In Islamic terms, they are more *jihadi* (in the combative and assertive meaning of the term) than *ijtihadi* in their approach to societal reconstruction and foreign policy.

The third attitude comes from neo-fundamentalist Islamists or those who adhere to a strict, literal interpretation of Islam, based on a particular school of thought emanating from particular Islamic scholars. What matters to them most is the text rather than the context. Without underestimating their diversity, on the whole they can be far more puritanical, sectarian, self-righteous, single-minded, discriminatory, xenophobic and coercive in their approach than the radical Islamists. Their preferred polity is mono-organizational, with a single leader exercising absolute power, closed to any form of pluralism, whether domestically grown or foreign inspired. They apply violence as a means not only to bring change but also to govern. In this sense, they are not much different from a variety of Marxist–Leninist totalitarian groups in the course of modern history. While their understanding of religion is basic, they are generally poorly educated but highly socialized in a particular religious setting. They are often popularly described as extremists or ultra-orthodox traditionalists. The Taliban militia and various Saudi-based Wahabi and Pakistan-based Muslim brotherhood and Deobandi groups, such as the Jamiat-e Ulema Islam (the Society of Learned Scholars) of Pakistan, are well known examples of this category.

Given the overlap between neo-fundamentalist and radical Islamist views, there have often been organic and organizational links between the two, with the latter using the former for human resources, protective purposes and outreach activities, including armed or terrorist operations. This was precisely the relationship between Al Qaeda and the Taliban, where Al Qaeda provided money and Arab fighters, and in return the Taliban harboured and helped Al Qaeda as a transnational force. This constituted a rare organic collaboration between Arab-led and non-Arab-led forces, their overlapping aspects reinforcing each other and assisting each to realize its objectives.

The fourth attitude stems from grassroots networks, whose knowledge of Islam is generally basic and at village and *madrasa* levels. They essentially follow Islam as a faith, and can be apolitical or political, depending on whether or not they feel their faith and way of life are threatened by hostile forces. Many of them are potential foot soldiers of Islam, vulnerable to manipulation by radical Islamists and neofundamentalists. They are often incapable of forming their own opinions about major political issues and events of the day, and remain very much at the mercy of what they learn from or are offered by the politically more informed and judgmental Islamists. They constitute the bulk of ordinary Muslims who, if left alone, could well remain preoccupied with their daily lives, especially in poor countries. However, they can be easily galvanized and mobilized by

Islamists and neofundamentalists, whether they live in poor suburbs or the countryside of Egypt or Pakistan. The plight of Muslims at the hands of 'foreigners' can rouse them to action. The Taliban recruited many of their foot soldiers from amongst such people. Their views of what happened on September 11 and its aftermath have been shaped by what they have been told by their local preachers and radical and neofundamentalist Islamist activists. Those views can range from intense dislike of the USA to indifference towards it.

The diverse attitudes towards Islam and Muslims in the West, and among Muslims towards the West, especially the USA, have caused much confusion and misunderstanding between the two sides. At the same time, while sharpened by the September 11 tragedy, these attitudes are grounded in a number of historical and contemporary issues which have been important in shaping them. Without a clear understanding of these issues, the crucial point of how Al Qaeda's actions came about will be missed in the debate, particularly in regard to the question of how to improve relations objectively and constructively between the West and the domain of Islam.

2

Shared Values and Conflicts: The Historical Experience

Since the advent of Islam in the early seventh century, relations between its domain and the largely Christian West have been marked by long periods of peaceful coexistence, but also by many instances of tension, hostility and mutual recrimination. Peaceful coexistence produced examples of majestic cooperation, tolerance and fruitful results in all fields of human endeavour, but the periods of tension were created or exploited by those elements from both sides that found deterioration of relations advantageous to their causes above and beyond religion. In today's world, it is not the peaceful coexistence and cooperation which is celebrated and built upon; rather, the tense and, at times, conflictual dimensions have come to determine the two sides' attitudes towards one another.

Islam and Christianity

Islam and Christianity, and for that matter Judaism, share much in terms of both beliefs and values. As the three main revealed monotheistic faiths, they not only embrace a common concept of God and His attributes, but also give equal weight to the sanctity of life as a precious gift from God. They are all rich in fundamental moral and social principles from which strong notions of universal ethics and justice can be drawn, and in relation to which a virtuous life can be organized on earth. In Islam, as in Christianity and Judaism, the notions of the power of God and vulnerability of man and woman as his creatures are combined to caution strongly against an earthly existence which defies God's commands and results in a life contrary to those principles that ensure a pious, truthful, just and communally acceptable living. One of the central elements of Christianity (and for that matter of Judaism) 'is [to] do justly, to love mercy, and to walk humbly with ... God'. Christianity has evolved to stress justice based on the principle that one must not do to others what one would not want others to do to you. This is akin to the Islamic principles, as enshrined in the Qur'an, that strongly emphasize the notion of justice as closest to piety, and the value of compassion, forgiveness, mercy, modesty, humility and persuasion as central to earthly existence to gain reward in the world hereafter. The Qur'an commands: 'O Ye who believe, be upright for God, witness injustice; and let not hatred of a people cause you to be unjust. Be just – that is closer to piety' (Sura v: 8).

Muslims are also guided by the Qur'anic command that they must respect all God's apostles and revealed books that came before Mohammed and the Qur'an. Muslims must treat respectfully the followers of these religions and provide them protection and freedom to follow their religion under Muslim rule. But Muslims must embrace Islam and its Prophet and book as final. Accordingly, an overwhelming majority of Muslims have historically been careful in their attitudes towards the followers of religions tolerated by the Qur'an, most importantly the Christians and Jews. Muslims have been restrained from engaging in the kind of pronouncements and actions that could insult or disparage such religions. Were they to do so, they would run contrary to Qur'anic commands and invite the wrath of God or Allah. The Qur'an states: 'Allah forbids you not, with regard to those who fight you not for (your) faith nor drive you out of your homes, from dealing kindly and justly with them: for Allah loveth those who are just' (Sura LX: 8).

This is not to claim that on the issue of dealings with peoples of other faiths, the Muslims are told always to turn the other cheek.[1] The Qur'an also contains injunctions that can easily be interpreted to justify belligerent actions towards them. For example, Sura IX has many such injunctions, where the command is to fight those who violate your religion and betray your trust, as is the case with: 'Fight those who believe not in Allah nor the Last Day, nor hold that forbidden which had been forbidden by Allah and His Apostle, nor acknowledge the religion of Truth, (even if they are) of the people of the Book, until they pay the Jizya with willing submission and feel themselves subdued' (Sura IX: 29). But such commands are either immediately or shortly thereafter qualified by assertions such as that God loves those who are kind and just and do good deeds by others.

Like the other two revealed religions, Islam puts a high premium on the value and sanctity of life. In Islam, only God, as creator and mover of the universe, is empowered to give and take life. The Qur'an commands that all Muslims be rewarded and punished according to their deeds on the Day of Judgement. This, however, does not preclude the notion of 'self-sacrifice' in the way of God or in defence of Islam. The Qur'an states: 'Nor take life – which Allah has made sacred – except For just cause. And if anyone is slain wrongfully, We have given his heir authority (to demand Qisas Or to forgive): but let him not exceed bounds in the matter of taking life: for he is helped (by the Law)' (Sura XVII: 33). This is also where the Islamic notion of martyrdom figures, as does Islam's endorsement of the concept of *jihad* – a concept which has often been invoked in history for a variety of both justifiable and unjustifiable reasons.

Jihad, which literally means struggle, effort and exertion, has had multiple meanings and methods of application in the course of Islamic history. The term has become complex and in many ways controversial. Various figures, movements and groups have invoked it for a variety of purposes (some with, others without, legitimate authority). In general, *jihad* carries 'the basic connotation of an endeavour toward a praiseworthy aim', including struggle against one's evil inclination or an exertion for the sake of Islam and Ummah (the Islamic domain).

There are basically two types of *jihad*: the greater *jihad* or personal, spiritual struggle; and lesser *jihad*, or the warfare form of struggle.[2] The Qur'an repeatedly reminds Muslims of the importance of the first form, as also often reinforced in the Sunna (the traditions of the Prophet Mohammed), without necessarily demeaning the value of the latter under the right circumstances. Yet what has in recent history gained popularity and received increased publicity is a tradition of the lesser *jihad* in the form of a 'holy war'. This is waged by Muslims when either their religion or their way of life and independence is seen as threatened or invaded. Various Islamist groups have invariably embraced this form of *jihad*. Most recently, these have ranged from the Afghan Islamic resistance forces (the Mujahideen) – a mixture of moderate and radical Islamists – which waged *jihad* against the Soviet occupation of Afghanistan in the 1980s and which were supported by the USA and its allies in a common cause, to the Palestinian Hamas, Lebanese Hezbullah or Kashmiri separatist Harakut al-Mujahideen.

Of course, Prophet Mohammed and his companions, who succeeded his religious and political leadership, engaged in many lesser *jihads*, but primarily to defend Islam and the Islamic community. As such, when they called for lesser *jihad*, they essentially called for a conceptually defensive act, proportionate to the Islamic emphasis on the sanctity of life – a concept of *jihad* that comes closest to what is described in Western literature as 'just war'.[3] The Qur'an commands: 'And fight in the way of God those who fight you, but do not commit aggression. God loved not the aggressors' (Sura II: 190). This is not to claim that defensive *jihad* has not on occasions involved offensive actions, but it is the defensive nature of *jihad* which is given primacy in Islam. In this case, Muslims are empowered only in a qualified sense to engage in self-sacrifice, without intending or actually harming non-combatant civilians of the opposite side.

It is important to emphasize that it is with reference to the notion of 'self-sacrifice' that the concept of martyrdom has also evolved in Islam. But not all forms of self-sacrifice result in martyrdom; only those carried out in defence of Islam, and when the defenders are killed by the enemy. If one engages in self-sacrifice for ends other than defence of Islam and if in the process one takes one's own life, it is suicide. This goes against the Islamic dictate concerning the sanctity of life and is therefore forbidden in Islam. As such, the notion of suicidal action to take one's own life and the lives of innocent non-combatants for political objectives has no place in the Islamic definition of *jihad* or martyrdom. It is regarded as morally and ethically repugnant when one deploys Islam to justify a political or politically motivated cause, no matter how compelling that cause is. In Islam, not every one can declare *jihad*. Only a learned religious authority (a scholar or jurist) that has reached the highest stage of *ijtihad* (independent reasoning) with widespread recognition in the Muslim world, and with the task of applying Sharia (Islamic Law) to contemporary circumstances can do so. Yet *ijtihad* itself has had a turbulent history in Islam.

Ijtihad was practised widely in the early centuries of Islam. In the fourteenth century, however, the leaders of Sunni Muslims, who constitute the majority sect in the domain of Islam (as against Shia or Shi'ite Muslims who are the majority only in Iran and Iraq) declared the 'gates of *ijtihad*' closed. They ordered scholars and jurists to use the legal decisions of past authorities instead of using their independent reasoning, which could give rise to creative interpretations of Islam in the application of Sharia. Many historians of Islam claim that this caused a major setback for Muslims: they could not apply Islam in a way relevant to the course of history, which in turn did not allow them to realize their full potential. They argue that this contributed markedly to preventing Muslims from keeping pace with those societal transformations which came to dominate Europe in the wake of the Renaissance. This was so especially in the realms of those ideas, values, practices and innovations that enabled European countries to leap forward. They contend that the failure of Muslims to catch up with many of these transformations in concurrence with, rather than in violation of, their religious beliefs and values enveloped the domain of Islam in the cloth of conservatism.[4] It thereby undermined its internal elasticity, dynamism, and ability to interact freely with, and benefit from, European liberalism, utilitarianism, empiricism and scientific and technological innovations.

Some moderate Islamists, who have become known as 'Islamic liberals' and come from both sides of the Sunni–Shia divide, take the issue further. They claim that the conservatism arising from closure of the gates of *ijtihad* reinforced the traditionalist view of the inseparability of religion and politics in Islam, at the cost of allowing the growth of another legitimate dimension of the faith. Their argument goes like this: Islam does not provide a theory of state and a clear blueprint as to what precisely an Islamic state should be. Prophet Mohammed left the application of Islam to the followers of Islam according to the changing conditions in the course of history, with the aid of four things that he left behind: the Qur'an, Sunna (the traditions of the Prophet), the example of his leadership and the original Islamic community. Islamic liberals even argue that the Prophet did not choose his religious and political successor deliberately because he wanted his followers to have a free choice in leadership and politics. They conclude from this that it is possible to have a secular state in a Muslim society. Two Islamic liberals who have moved in this direction in recent times, although with different emphasis, are Abdurrahman Wahid of Indonesia and Mohammed Khatami of Iran. After coming to power in 1997 through democratic procedures, Wahid made it abundantly clear that he considered it legitimate to have secular politics in a predominantly Muslim Indonesia. Khatami, who has been elected to the presidency of Iran twice in landslide victories since 1997, has argued that Islam is compatible with democracy, and has pushed for the creation of 'Islamic civil society' and 'Islamic democracy', which in their manifestations are the same as those in the West. (This issue is discussed in detail in Chapter 4.)

The closure of the gates of *ijtihad* challenged many Muslim thinkers and activists over the centuries, more especially from the late nineteenth century. Many Islamic figures sought to undo the fourteenth-century decision, but none more assertively than such Islamists of modern times as Sayyed Jamal al-Afghani, Maulana Alama Iqbal of Indo-Pakistan, Abul Ala Mawdudi of Pakistan, Ayatollah Khomeini, Ali Shariati, and Mohammed Khatami of Iran and Mohammed Abdu', Sayyed Qutb of Egypt, and Abdurrahman Wahid of Indonesia. Notwithstanding their political stance and attitudes towards the West, their exemplary efforts in seeking to reopen the door of *ijtihad* have entitled them to be called the modern Mujtahideen (practitioners of *ijtihad*) of Islam. Their *ijtihadi* interpretation and application of Islam have had a profound impact on the ideological and political landscape of various parts of the domain of Islam, more specifically various movements and groups spawned by their influence.

Generally, in Islam two kinds of approaches, each with many variants, have historically developed towards understanding and using the shared values of Islam, Christianity and Judaism, and the multi-meaning concept of *jihad*: *jihadi* and *ijtihadi*. These two terms have been deployed intermittently to achieve different textual and contextual results. They have been drawn upon to justify a variety of *jihadi* or combative approaches to incite extremism and conflict between the domain of Islam and the West. Or alternatively they have been liberally interpreted to promote *ijtihadi* causes, such as interfaith and inter-civilizational dialogues, positive interactions and cooperation, and reasons for coexistence based on a non-competitive and non-combative notion of justice and moral existence. The history of relations between the domain of Islam and the West bears witness to both, although with the *ijtihadi* dimension spanning a much longer period than has the *jihadi* dimension – an issue which deserves to be looked at in detail.

Peaceful Coexistence

Undoubtedly, common features and supporting Islamic ordinances played a significant role in fostering a period of highly tolerant coexistence among Muslims, Jews and Christians during the first five centuries of Islam. Despite original Jewish and Christian resistance to Mohammed's claim of prophecy in Mecca from 612, and the tension and hostility that this engendered between the followers of Mohammed and those of the other two religions, Mohammed persisted with preaching principles of tolerance, persuasion and cooperation as against warfare and bloodshed. This was instrumental in fostering bridges of understanding and trust between the followers of the three faiths. Even when Islam's march of expansion beyond the Arabian peninsula took off following Mohammed's death in 632, creating a vast empire of faith, grafted on various cultures and ethnicities, within a century of Islam's birth, Islam maintained its pristine respect for other revealed religions and interacted with them positively and dialectically. This is not to claim that there were no acts of violence and assertion of religious superiority, but many Jewish and Christian communities that came under the rule of Islam were on the whole provided protection, albeit in return for a tax payment, and allowed to live free of any religious persecution. These qualities were manifested prominently and critically in the wake of the Islamic conquest of Jerusalem in the mid-630s as they were in the subsequent Islamic reign of the Abbassids (750–1250). Under the 'Omar agreement', named after the second Caliph (ruler) of Islam, Omar Ibn al-Khitab, the Arab Muslim forces established Muslim political rule over the city but accorded full recognition to the right to freedom of religion for Jews and Christians in Jerusalem. The employment of Jewish, and Christian and many other non-Muslim thinkers, scholars and professionals in the court of the Abbassids, as equals alongside their Muslim counterparts, marked the height of this development.

Jonathan Bloom and Sheila Blair write:

> In the Islamic lands, not only Muslims but also Christians and Jews enjoyed the good life. They dressed in fine clothing, had fine houses in splendid cities serviced by paved streets, running water, and sewers and dined on spiced delicacies served on Chinese porcelains. Seated on luxurious carpets, these sophisticated city dwellers debated such subjects as the nature of God, the intricacies of Greek philosophy, or the latest Indian mathematics. Muslims considered this Golden Age God's reward to mankind for spreading His faith and His speech over the world.[5]

It was largely in this context that Islam motivated the development of a great Arab Islamic empire, with a very vibrant, dynamic civilization – a civilization which was based not only on what it cherished from Islam and Arabs, and the indissoluble bonds between the two, but also, in 'a give and take' manner that profited from other religions and cultures. Islam's rejection of race, ethnicity, colour and any form of compartmentalization of life, its tolerance of other religions, and treatment of Muslims, Christians and Jews as all the children of Abraham opened the door to a variety of peoples, including those who did not embrace it, to live in its domain with protection and dignity, and participate and contribute to its achievements and be rewarded for them.

This is not to claim that all the co-religionists lived in perfect harmony at all times, but it does indicate that a remarkable degree of peaceful coexistence, mutual respect and tolerance prevailed among them. At the time, the Jewish biblical claim to Palestine as their 'promised land' was not markedly pronounced, and the Arab Muslims' rule of Palestine and their imperial dominance did not cause many Jews or Christians to feel ostracized. The Jewish claim that they are the divinely chosen people, the Christians' claim of precedence over Islam, and Islam's exaltation of an authoritative nature as the seal of all revealed faiths played no major role in overriding the co-religionists' shared values and largely harmonious coexistence. There was no systematic persecution of followers of other revealed religions, and holy wars were strictly within the province of the Caliphs as the last resort to defend the Islamic faith and its domain. Not every man of distinction was empowered to call for a *jihad*.

However, the situation changed with the Christian Crusades and subsequent Western colonial and imperialist encroachment upon the Muslim world. The Crusades against Muslims, the Crusaders' capture of Jerusalem twice between 1099 and 1229, and the final recapture of the city by Muslims by the mid-thirteenth century left lasting imprints of distrust and residual enmity between many of the orthodox followers of these religions. The Crusaders were spectacularly severe in capturing Jerusalem in 1100. They not only brutalized and humiliated the Arab Muslim citizens of Jerusalem, but also made the Jewish inhabitants of the city suffer to the extent that many of them felt they had more to fear from the Christians than from their traditional Muslim rulers. Although the Muslims eventually dislodged the

Crusaders, the whole incident changed the favourable view that Muslims had held so far of Christians, and many Muslims remained wary of them for a long time to come.

Even so, this still did not lead to any assault by Muslims on Christianity, which they continued to respect as a religion of the Book sanctioned by the Qur'an. This attitude prevailed long after the decline of Abbassids into the periods of their Turkic successors. Under Ottoman imperial Islamic rule (1350–1918), the situation by and large remained contained, with an effort not to ostracize Christian communities within the empire because of the Crusaders' activities. Certainly, the Ottomans saw themselves as the protectors of the Sunni Islamic faith against Christendom to the West and Shia Safavid Persia to the east of their empire, and for this they mounted *jihads*, which resulted in territorial expansion and the spread of Islam into eastern and southern Europe, and in numerous wars with the Safavids. Yet they retained for the most part the ethos of respect for and decent treatment of non-Muslims under their rule. After bringing the whole of Syria and Egypt under their rule, and incorporating North Africa and Arabia into the empire, they pressed on. Karen Armstrong writes:

> The Ottoman armies continued their conquest of Europe and reached the gates of Vienna in the 1530s. The sultans now ruled a massive empire, with superb bureaucratic efficiency, unrivalled by any other state at this time. The sultan did not impose uniformity on his subjects nor did he try to force the disparate elements of his empire into one huge party. The government merely provided a framework which enabled the different groups – Christians, Jews, Arabs, Turks, Berbers, merchants, *ulema*, *tariqahs* and trade guilds – to live together peacefully, each making its own contribution, and following its own beliefs and customs.[6]

Even when, by the eighteenth century, the Ottoman Empire weakened towards its eventual demise (largely due to conservatism, internal decay, imperial overstretch, and inability to keep pace with European innovations and defend itself effectively against rising European powers), the followers of non-Islamic faiths were still not subjected to any noticeable degree of persecution or forceful methods of conversion. As the conservative *ulema*, who promoted non-*ijtihadi* views of Islam, grew increasingly opposed to the European Enlightenment and education, scientific and technological innovations, the Christian and Jewish co-religionists enjoyed by and large a peaceful and cooperative life under the Ottoman rulers. Most of the orthodox Christians who fled into the Holy Roman Empire during the Turkish invasion of the Balkans after the fall of Constantinople in 1453, returned within 20 years, because they heard from those who had stayed behind that they were free to practise their religion and were not pressured to convert to Islam, whereas those who had fled were constantly pressured to convert to Catholicism. The Ottoman system of *millet* (territorial division along ethnic and religious lines) and *janissaries* (the Sultan's elite troops) served them well, although the Janissaries were composed of those who had been taken as children from Christian families in the Balkans, then brought up as Muslims – a practice abolished in 1827 after the Janissaries mutinied.

Colonialism and Islamic Responses

Nonetheless, Western (especially British and French) colonialism, following the start of European expansionism from the sixteenth century, altered the picture. The rise of the Western powers, with a resolve to conquer other domains for 'civilizing', mercantile, terri-torial and geopolitical purposes, made the Muslim territories of the Ottoman Empire, especially those en route to the Indian subcontinent, Far East and Southeast Asia, fair game. From the late eighteenth century, the French, Spanish, Italians and British made inroads into North Africa, the British into the Persian Gulf to secure bases and protect their sea lanes, and as a result all started nibbling away different parts of a weakening Ottoman Empire, especially at the edges. Further afield still, the Russians encroached on the northeast of the Islamic world in Transcaucasus and Central Asia, and the British and Dutch on its south-east extremities in Malaya and the East Indies. This simply reinforced among the Muslims the painful residue of the Crusades. It caused wider humiliation for them as many of their communities in North Africa, the Middle East, Transcaucasus, Central, South and Southeast Asia fell one after another to colonial domination and cultural suppression.

The colonial subjugation of the Arab domain and many other parts of the Muslim world was viewed by many Muslims as a Christian onslaught against their identity, religion, culture and way of life.

It contributed substantially to bifurcation of the subjected Muslim societies into secularist elites and Islamic clusters. The former, who become imbued with Western ideals, education and social and cultural practices, embraced the goal of modernization, along Western lines, to transform their societies. Although some saw this modernization as a necessary prelude to confronting the colonialists, other secularist elites, whether in Egypt, Algeria, Indonesia or Malaya, were adopted or backed by colonial powers who provided them with internal mechanisms of control and postcolonial influence. The Islamic clusters, on the other hand, emerged in many instances as a reaction to the push by the colonial powers and their indigenous allies for secularization of Muslim societies. They devoted themselves to reforming and reorganizing their communities according to Islamic teachings. They surfaced in different shades, intensity and with a variety of approaches, although all within an Islamic framework, to challenge colonial powers or their local allies and pro-Western modernity.

Some of the Islamic elements were decidedly puritanical, calling for a return to the basic teachings and values of Islam as enshrined, in their view, in the Qur'an and Hadith; some even advocated extremism as the medium for change. They were either followers of, or influenced by, the medieval Islamic reformer Ibn Tammiyyah (1263–1328), whose Islamic tradition has historically grown to become a valuable source for Islamic militancy. One of the prominent early examples of this cluster was Mohammed ibn Abd al-Wahab (1703–87) of the Arabian peninsula, the founder of the Wahabi movement, which through an alliance with the ruling Ibn Saud dynasty continues to be a central player in the politics and society of the modern Saudi state. Although initially the Wahabi movement emerged in the context of tribal rivalries in Arabia and against Ottoman rule of the holy cities of Mecca and Medina, one of its objectives was to oppose secularization and Westernization of the peninsula. It certainly succeeded in blocking the path of secularization, if not pro-Western modernization, in what eventually emerged as the Kingdom of Saudi Arabia.

Another example of this clustering were Mahdists or followers of those Islamic leaders who claimed to be Mahdis (the 'divinely guided' or 'awaited' ones sent by God) and who mounted revolts against European colonialism in different parts of the Muslim domain. They too essentially wanted a return to what they regarded as the true and uncorrupted Islam as opposed to European political and cultural hegemony. One who proclaimed himself the Mahdi, with a mission to liberate the Sudanese in particular, and the Muslims in general from colonialist rule, was Mohammed Ahmad ibn Abdullah. He rose from Northern Sudan in 1881 and declared a *jihad* against the British and their Egyptian allies. His followers succeeded in defeating several British led Egyptian armies, and in 1885 captured Khartoum and killed the British General Gordon.[7] His rule did not last very long, as he died in 1886, and his successor Khalifa Abdallahi ruled only until 1898, when the British defeated him at Omdurman and regained control of Sudan; however, his tradition of Puritanism and Islamic resistance to outside domination became a recurring event in the Muslim world.

A different strand of the Islamic clusters that emerged concerned those who were associated with Islamic Sufism or mysticism. This cluster wanted to achieve more or less what their orthodox puritanical counterparts advocated, but they pursued a different approach. Prominent among them was the Moroccan Sufi reformer Ahmad ibn Idris (1780–1836), who emphasized the importance of education, but nonetheless rejected Western influences. Another was the neo-Sufi Mohammed ibn Ali al-Sanusi (d. 1832), who found the Sanusiayyah movement, which remains the dominant form of Islam in Libya to date.

Another cluster demonstrably relied on what they could blend from the West as good and compatible with Islam in order to rejuvenate Islam as an ideology of salvation, reform, renewal, mobilization and resistance in deference to changing times and conditions. This cluster wanted to unite and galvanize Muslims first to understand their religion aright and reform the Muslim domain from within as virtually a prerequisite for meeting the challenges posed by colonialism and its associated secularization and Westernization. The Islamic leaders who pioneered this cluster were Sayyed Jamal al-Afghani, the advocate of a pan-Islamic movement in the second half of the nineteenth century, and Hassan al-Banna, founder of the Muslim Brotherhood, in the first half of the twentieth century.

Al-Afghani (1839–97), whose origins are disputed between Afghanistan and Iran, was a remarkable, though controversial, *ijtihadi* Islamic thinker and activist of his time, well versed not only in the Muslim world, but also in Europe.[8] He made a pioneer effort to straddle the Sunni–Shia divide and crisscross the domain of Islam in order to reenergize and unite Muslims, primarily for two

purposes: internal reform (*islah*) and renewal (*tajdid*), and resistance
to European, more specifically British, colonialism. He saw nothing
wrong with Muslims adopting what was good from European scientific and technological achievements and using this to advance in all
fields of human endeavour. He argued that Islam was not hostile to
science and technology, but he shunned the power of the West,
expressed fear about the West crushing the Muslim world, and urged
Muslims to unite and progress as the best way to defend themselves
and their religion against colonialism. His zeal for reform, renewal
and resistance at times took him to the border of extremist actions;
he was accused of being behind the assassination of a Persian Qajar
king in the 1890s, in order to support the cause of constitutionalism
in Persia. However, despite mounting a vigorous Islamic-based
ideological and politically combative campaign against Western
domination, al-Afghani's achievements in practical terms were
limited. He died a frustrated reformer and anti-colonial campaigner,
but he left behind a number of distinguished followers.

One of them was the Mufti of Egypt, Mohammed Abdu
(1849–1905), who was a seasoned and shrewd Islamic thinker. While
in some ways like al-Afghani, impressed by the political, legal and
educational institutions of the West and feeling very much at home
in Europe and with Europeans, he intensely disliked British colonial
control of Egypt. Yet, he had no time for any kind of Islamic militancy either. He sought Egypt's freedom and its transformation into
a modern Islamic state through an evolutionary process of change, in
which education, not extremism, would play a central role. He wanted
the implementation of Sharia as a source of reform and democracy,
but at the same time was well disposed towards wedding the Islamic
tradition with that of the West to achieve his objectives. Then again,
like al-Afghani, Abdu had to contend with little change as far as the
British occupation of his country was concerned. But the impact of
al-Afghani and Abdu influenced a future generation of reformist
Islamic thinkers and activists in coming decades.

Hassan al-Banna (1906–49), an Egyptian teacher, emerged as one
of the most prominent and effective members of his generation to
build on some of al-Afghani's and Abdu's ideas. Pained by British
control of Egypt and Western domination of the Muslim world, and
the rising level of poverty and backwardness in Egypt and elsewhere
in that world, he called for Islamic spiritual reformation, rejuvenation
and modernization, as well as the solidarity of the Muslim Ummah

along Sharia lines. While rejecting any notion of separation of religion and politics in Islam, he stressed the need for modern education to enable Muslims to acquire what was good in the fields of science, technology, industry and social welfare, and what was needed to reform their political and social institutions. In the 1920s he founded the Society of Ikhwan ul-Muslimun (Muslim Brotherhood), which rapidly developed into a major movement, claiming membership and influence well beyond Egypt.

The Muslim Brotherhood was a religious, political and social movement. It engaged not only in educating Brothers and Sisters in Islam, but also in providing modern education, social services, schools, clinics and hospitals in rural areas, factories, and other facilities to help raise public awareness and the standard of living with a view to constructing a modern society in Egypt as a prelude to helping the transformation and liberation of the Ummah as a whole. It even set up health insurance, and educated Muslims in modern labour laws so that they could defend themselves against exploitation and deprivation imposed by the colonial powers and their indigenous allies.[9] It essentially acted as an alternative government, providing services where the government was very weak or had failed. This practice was emulated by several groups, under the Brothers' influence, which cropped up in the Muslim Middle East a generation later – an issue discussed in Chapter 4.

Although al-Banna died in 1949 and the authorities' reaction to the activities of a few of his extremist followers took a toll on his organization, the Muslim Brotherhood went on to become a mass movement, with some two million members by the late 1940s in Egypt and beyond. Its cells sprang up in many parts of the Muslim world, from Palestine to Pakistan. One of its most influential followers who emerged was Abul Ala Mawdudi (1903–79), who after the partition of the Indian subcontinent in 1947 into predominantly Hindu India and mostly Muslim Pakistan, took up residence in Pakistan. Mawdudi opposed secularization and Western domination, and called for unity of Muslims against these two phenomena. He essentially proposed an 'Islamic liberation theology', and inspired thousands to wage *jihad* against both internal ignorance and foreign influence.[10] He established the Jamaat-i Islami (Islamic Societies) in Pakistan, and affected Pakistani politics to the extent that in the constitution of 1956 the country was described as an 'Islamic republic', the first of its kind in the Muslim world. His followers gained disproportionate political influence in relation to their numerical strength in the context of Pakistan's re-Islamization under the military dictatorship of General Zia ul-Haq (1977–88), and Pakistan's support of the Afghan Islamic resistance forces (the Mujahideen) to the Soviet occupation of Afghanistan in the 1980s. Despite the fact that they failed to win a single seat in any post-Zia ul-Haq elections, they still managed to display a great deal of prowess.

These developments were also echoed in the eastern end of the Muslim domain, that is the Indonesia archipelago or East Indies under Dutch colonial rule. By the turn of the twentieth century, Reform Islam, which essentially stood for religious renewal and emphasized the need for wider religious education among the majority of the archipelago's people, with an embrace of the goal of modern-ization, appeared firmly on the political and social landscape. Of course, given the social and cultural diversity of the archipelago, the advocates of Reform Islam were careful to keep in step with the arch-ipelago's circumstances; it was devoid of some of the radicalism of its Middle Eastern counterparts at the time. By the second decade of the century, Reform Islam had spawned various groups. The most important ones were Sarekat Islam and Muhammadiyah – both founded in 1912 by the same social group of reformist Islam, although with the former stressing economic interests and the latter religiosity as the basis for political and social transformation of the Indonesia archipelago. They found their strength in different islands, with Muhammadiyah making a strong inroad into Aceh, which has lately emerged as Indonesia's main centre for Islamic militancy.

It was from Sarekat Islam, however, that the most influential Islamic social organization, Nahdatul Ulama (NU), originated in 1926. The NU grew rapidly as a mass Islamic traditionalist move-ment to strengthen relations among *ulema* and various Sunni schools, to spread Islamic education, make sure that educational textbooks conformed to Islamic values, and to provide religious and social services. By the turn of the 1940s, NU came to share the anticolo-nialism emphasis of many of its Middle Eastern and South Asian counterparts, cooperated with the Japanese to achieve Indonesian independence under Sukarno's leadership in 1945, and demanded parliamentary representation for the Indonesian people. In the elec-tion of 1955, it secured some 18 per cent of the national vote, but its relations with Sukarno's regime soured, partly due to the activities of pro-Chinese communists. In the 1965 change of power, NU sided with General Suharto, only to change posture by the early 1980s to serve as a strong critic of Suharto's dictatorship. This also coincided with the organization's election of Abdurrahman Wahid, who subsequently became President of Indonesia (1999–2001), as the chair of its executive council. NU today claims some 30–40 million members.

However, these globally dispersed Islamic movements and organizations ultimately failed to achieve their common goal of uniting Muslims against internal decay and outside intervention and subjugation. With the partial exception of the Muslim Brothers, none could claim more than local impact. Their significance lay not so much in what they achieved as in what they fostered as a new Islamic awakening among Muslims, which would gain deeper and wider salience under appropriate conditions with Israel's territorial expansion in the wake of the 1967 Arab–Israeli war, the Iranian revolution of 1978–79 and the Soviet invasion of Afghanistan in December 1979 – issues which are discussed in full in Chapter 4. What prevailed against colonial rule of and encroachments upon the domain of Islam was the rising tide of nation state based secular nationalism (itself a European importation), led in many cases by members of the very Western-inspired elites on which the colonial powers had relied as the mechanisms of their rule and influence.

Secular Responses

The man who first embodied this was the Turkish leader, Mustafa Kemal Ataturk (1881–1938), a distinguished general, secular nationalist and reformer, who struggled against the European powers and established the independent state of Turkey out of the ruins of the Ottoman Empire in the wake of the First World War. Ataturk moved both judiciously and forcefully to take Islam out of politics and discard traditions, with a clear aim of transforming Turkey along European lines.[11] He proved popular at home, but he also struck a chord with many other Western-inspired leaders elsewhere in the Muslim world. Two of his contemporaries were Reza Khan, who took over power in Iran in 1921 and replaced the traditional Qajar dynasty with his own Pahlavi dynastical rule in 1925, and King Amanullah Khan, who assumed the throne of Afghanistan in 1919 – the year in which he also declared Afghanistan's full independence from Great Britain.[12]

Both Reza Khan, who after assumption of the throne became Reza Shah, and Amanullah were deeply impressed and influenced by Ataturk, and sought to duplicate many of his reforms in their own countries, although in their secularist dispositions neither could go as far as Ataturk, given their different national conditions and geopolitical circumstances. Amanullah's reformist rule, which was opposed by the British, produced a serious popular backlash from the deeply conservative and ethno-tribalized Afghan people, resulting in his overthrow in 1929 and the reversal of many of his reforms. Reza Shah's rule was confronted by serious opposition from both Iran's Shi'ite establishment and its pro-democracy elements. However, it was his nationalist stand to forge close ties with Hitler's Germany as the only power capable of counter-balancing the traditional Anglo–Russian rivalry over Iran that proved unpalatable to the Allied powers during the Second World War. British and Soviet forces jointly invaded Iran in 1941, forcing Reza Shah to abdicate in favour of his young and inexperienced son, Mohammed Reza Pahlavi, who suited the purpose of the Allies. Even so, the age of reformism, secularism and nationalism continued to sweep the domain of Islam, limiting and moderating the behaviour of Islamic forces and preventing them from gaining power, at the risk of galvanizing and exploiting popular resentment that Western colonialism had generated, thus poisoning relations with the West.

As the age of post-Second World War decolonization settled in, again it was the nationalist, secularist elites, not the Islamic ones, which took over the reins of many Muslim countries. This was so whether in Indonesia under Sukarno or Egypt under Gamal Abdul Nasser, Algeria under Ben Bella or for that matter many other Muslim countries. Saudi Arabia was the only country within the domain of Islam which at this time had experienced Islamic rule of a kind and continued to do so in the following decades, but in close alliance with the West, especially the USA. If differences and antagonism developed between some of the Muslim countries and the West, they had more political and nationalist than religious bases. The talk was not of a *jihad* against the West, but rather political and cultural freedom from the West and economic and technological accommodation with the West. In fact, by the 1950s and 1960s, except for Saudi Arabia, there was not a single Muslim country overtly ruled by an Islamic force. What, by and large, prevailed was the political ascendancy of secularist forces in the Muslim domain. This is not to suggest that all these forces were necessarily pro-Western. Far from it: many of them were steering nationalist courses of behaviour, and were inclined to take advantage of the global Cold War between the two rival super-powers, the USA and the Soviet Union, to entrench such behaviour. However, what it does reveal is that opposition on the part of some of them stemmed not from a religious stand but rather from secular nationalist and ideological pursuits. This raises the fundamental question: what happened that generated the necessary conditions to give rise to Islamism, in some cases with extremist tendencies, as a potent political force for change in many parts of the Muslim world? Did it have much to do with the rise of the USA to globalism and its policy behaviour towards the domain of Islam?

3

US Globalism and Regional Domination

The rise of the USA to the status of global superpower following the Second World War proved a double-edged phenomenon for Muslims. On the one hand, it helped them to free themselves from European colonial rule, which emerged greatly weakened in the wake of the war. On the other, it confronted them with difficult choices, especially in the context of American–Soviet Cold War rivalry. They now had to come to terms with a new world situation dominated, from the standpoint of many of them, by either Godless Soviet socialism or American anti-Soviet benevolent hegemonism. This was punctuated by a phase of decolonization, opening the way for those of them that were still colonized to achieve independence and pursue modernization. In the process, while some looked to the Soviet Union, some to the USA, and some adopted a variety of neutral nationalist postures, most of them could not strike an easy balance between the requirements of modernization to ameliorate their living conditions and protect their freedom and independence, and what was required to maintain their Muslim identity and way of life. Many of them drifted towards different types of authoritarian and often corrupt and incompetent regimes, with no appropriate national ideology or agenda of reform and renewal. Amid confusion and searching for security, some of them saw Soviet influence or 'non-alignment' as a means to overcome their colonial past, while others embraced the USA.

However, neither the first category, including such countries as Afghanistan, Egypt, Indonesia and Somalia, nor the second category, including such states as Iran and Pakistan, found their experiences painless. They discovered that what really mattered to the two superpowers were their own ideological tussle and determination to defeat one another. They found themselves simply pawns in a global game in which they could play little or no role unless they attached themselves to one of the rival powers, or achieved the ability to play off the two powers in order to have a degree of autonomy in conducting their domestic and foreign policies. The interactive dynamism between external pressure and domestic failure eroded the capacity of many of them to reform internally. They could neither deflect exogenous pressures, nor pursue what could ensure their progress and well-being, without generating the necessary conditions for extremist political and religious backlashes.

Yet by the 1960s, when only Saudi Arabia was under a specifically Islamic government and Pakistan – another US ally – was flirting with the idea, both residual anticolonial feelings and frustration from domestic failures had come to intersect with what was seen in many Muslim countries as US hegemonic behaviour. As the USA remained overly focused on its anti-communism crusade and less than sensitive to the consequences of its penetration of various parts of the Muslim domain in pursuing this crusade, seeds of serious dissatisfaction with the USA and what was 'American' were rapidly germinating among segments of Muslim populations, from Iran to Egypt to Indonesia. Many Muslim nationalists, Arab and non-Arab, had begun to view American globalist quests for influence in the Muslim world as a follow-up to, if not exactly an extension of, European colonialism, and after the foundation of Israel in 1948, as also linked to Zionism. Two issues need to be looked at closely and interrelatedly: where did American globalism impact most in Islam's domain, and to what extent did it contribute to generating anti-Americanism there?

Early US Involvement

In any study of US involvement in the vast and diverse Muslim domain, three points need emphasis. The first is that US interests there predated the Second World War. The second is that the most forceful phase of America's penetration of key parts of the domain came after that war, in the context of America's campaign to contain Soviet communism through a Cold War, which brought a 'long peace' to Europe or 'the North' but several wars as part of what can be called a 'long war' in the South, involving most of the Muslim domain's Asia–Middle East components. The third is that the growth of US involvement and dominance in the Muslim domain was facilitated by the failure of ruling elites in many parts of it to build appropriate domestic structures and processes to cushion them against increased vulnerability to outside interference. This failure helped generate a vicious cycle, whereby domestic weaknesses and foreign pressure kept feeding one another, creating growing volatility and instability in the domain.

The USA was not a participant in European colonialism and has therefore not been generally seen as a colonial power – a feature that has historically made it attractive as an ally to many Muslim societies, independent or colonized. Despite its expansion within the North American continent and its southward-oriented hegemonic aspirations, the USA for more than a century after independence from Britain remained quite isolationist in relation to the world at large. It generally took cover from the security and diplomatic shield provided by Great Britain in global affairs; and as a former colony itself, it felt no compulsion to venture outside its domain for territorial acquisition.

However, this did not last beyond the nineteenth century. In an age of a growing European 'colonial grab' for Afro–Asian territories, US foreign policy came under increasing pressure by the 1890s from two clusters in Washington: the 'Hamiltonians' who had developed strong colonial urges for patriotic, neomercantilist and great power status reasons, and were calling for the building of a blue water navy and adventures on the high seas; and the 'Jeffersonians', who argued for strong coastal defences but against colonial territorial acquisitions.[1] As the former gained the upper hand, a fever of foreign policy assertiveness seized President William McKinley's Administration. In 1898, the USA fought Spain over Cuba, and the American Asiatic fleet ventured into the Pacific, not just to defeat the Spanish navy in the Bay of Manila but also to take over the Philippines, acquisition of which, together with Puerto Rico, the Hawaiian Islands, Guam and Samoa, amounted to a colonial-imperialist grab for self-glorification and enrichment.

Meanwhile, in 1903, US Secretary of State John Hay issued what became known as his 'Open Door' notes, calling for preservation of China's territorial and administrative integrity against all those powers – Russia, Britain, Germany, France and Japan – which in practice were set on dividing China into spheres of influence. This act, accompanied with a growing degree of assertiveness toward other rival powers over China, so as to keep especially the Russians and Japanese at bay, and prompt the European powers to play fairly, marked a change in Washington's foreign policy behaviour. The McKinley Administration, with Theodore Roosevelt (later President) as its Assistant Secretary of Defense, moved to expand American involvement in global affairs. Although initially constrained by domestic considerations and by Washington's continued deference to Britain as a valuable maritime ally, the onset of the First World War, among other things, helped propel the USA closer to a leadership role in the Asian–Middle Eastern theatre.

The United States' entry into the First World War, primarily in support of Britain and its wartime allies against Germany, Austria-Hungary and Turkey; the subsequent triumph of revolutionary Bolsheviks in Russia in 1917; the breakup of the Ottoman Empire; and concurrent consolidation of the British government's hold on the Iranian oil industry, provided the USA with further opportunities to widen its involvement. The war proved very costly for the European powers, Britain in particular, without necessarily blocking the path for Germany to reemerge as a significant power, and Japan to continue emerging.

Britain, which had already experienced a sharp industrial decline relative to Germany since the last quarter of the nineteenth century, was experiencing overstretch of its resources. It could no longer cope effectively with the new challenge posed by the Bolsheviks and pressure from a rising tide of anticolonial nationalism in its Asian–Middle Eastern colonies.

While not a party to the Treaty of Versailles (1919), and therefore not restricted by its obligations, Washington not only became more critical of Japan and Germany and a vigilant watcher of Soviet behaviour during the inter-war period; it also moved steadily to enlarge its own geopolitical interests, often in competition with, and at the expense of, European powers. Oil soon provided a major focus around which the USA could build its post-First World War activities in the Muslim Middle East.

Oil in commercial quantities had already been discovered in predominantly Shia Muslim Persia by the turn of the twentieth century, and the British Burmah Oil Company (later British Petroleum Company – BP) and British government soon gained full control over it, turning it by the 1920s into a highly profitable business. This added an important new dimension, not only to traditional Anglo–Russian rivalry, as the Soviets now tried, unsuccessfully, to secure a share in Iran's oil wealth, but also to Anglo–American relations. As the world learned more about the value of oil as a significant, long-term source of energy, American oil companies were increasingly motivated to push for a share in prospecting and exploiting overseas resources. But they were confronted by the British monopoly of Persian oil and political dominance in the region.[2]

However, they did not need to wait long to make an inroad. The USA found its first strategic foothold in Saudi Arabia under King Abdul Aziz. He had used a mixture of Islam and British support to consolidate his hold on Islam's most holy land since 1902, and to establish a Wahabi Islamic government, which was both theocratic and autocratic, with a degree of openness to the West to secure an external source of security against his domestic and regional opponents. Thus from the start, the relationship between King Abdul Aziz and the USA found primacy in the King's need for security and America's interests in oil and strategic gains. It developed on the basis of mutual convenience: neither Saudi Islamic fundamentalism nor American secularist democracy figured as an issue in the relationship. In 1933, King Abdul Aziz gave Jimmy Moffett, a personal friend of Franklin D. Roosevelt and head of a Californian oil company, the first concession to prospect and exploit oil in his newly proclaimed independent kingdom. Moffett's success in discovering the first big deposit in 1937, and commencing the export of Saudi oil a year later, marked a turning point.

Given the close relations between the US government and the American oil companies, which Washington subsequently identified as instruments of American foreign policy, control of Saudi oil laid a solid foundation for the USA to pursue wider economic and strategic involvement in the region. It was also shortly after the flow of Saudi oil had begun that a report was submitted to President Roosevelt by an American commission of experts which firmly drew his attention to the fact that the centre of gravity of the world's petroleum output was shifting to the Persian Gulf. By the early 1940s, President Roosevelt found it expedient to develop a close friendship with the conservative King Abdul Aziz. While showing no political or moral qualms over the theocratic character of the Saudi regime, Roosevelt committed the USA secretly, though incrementally, to Saudi Arabia's security and defence, with a firm resolve to expand the sphere of American activities in the region.

Oil-rich Iran became the next immediate target, irrespective of its historical sectarian differences and political rivalries with the Arabs.

Whereas in the past Washington had deflected Iranian approaches for close ties to counter the traditional Anglo–Soviet rivalry, by the early 1940s it seemed to have little hesitation in capitalizing on Iranian goodwill to expand relations. In late 1941, after Iran was jointly occupied by the Second World War allies Britain and the USSR, with US support (primarily to open a corridor for supplying the Soviet Union in the war against Germany, and to check German influence), the State Department appealed to American missionary schools in Iran to 'keep up their good work' of countering 'bad influences' there. It advocated resumption of trade negotiations with Iran, for reasons of political expediency, to safeguard American trade interests there for after the war, and to ensure that 'American oil companies interested in Iran could be welcomed in the region'.[3]

The USA also bolstered its military mission in Iran, to expedite Lend-Lease shipments to the Soviet Union, by dispatching additional military experts and advisors to the Iranian government. In response to an Iranian request in 1943, an American financial mission, headed by Arthur C. Millspaugh, was sent to reorganize Iran's financial system. In February 1944, Washington raised its Legation to Embassy status, and came out publicly in full support of Iran remaining an independent sovereign state, with a democratic government and free enterprise system in the postwar era.

From this point, the USA also dropped most of the inhibitions that had previously prompted it not to encroach upon British interests in the area. While providing support during 1942–43 to the British from its Persian Gulf Command, of about 30,000 troops, Washington ensured that the assistance it provided would support its goal of broadening its long-term involvement in the region. For example, when the British requested Lend-Lease funds to build several pipelines across Iran, Washington asked for assurances that the pipelines would be made available to American companies after the war. This was followed in the first half of 1944 by Washington's tacit backing, without consulting either the British or the Soviets, of an approach to the Iranian government for oil concessions by two American oil companies, Standard Vacuum and Sinclair. Irritated by this American action, both powers objected strongly – the Soviets loudly and clearly, the British quietly and diplomatically. When the Soviets demanded similar concessions, the Iranian parliament passed a bill banning oil concessions to anyone while allied forces remained in Iran. The Soviets, who suspected the Iranian government of collusion with the USA and Britain, denounced the decision as a 'disloyal and unfriendly' act; but the Americans declared it within the 'sovereign right of Iran'.[4] The British, however, had reasons to be pleased about the Iranian decision, but not for long.

Washington maintained an increasingly high profile on the changing national circumstances of Iran. When, contrary to a 1942 agreement with the British and Iranian governments, the Soviets did not withdraw their troops from Iran within six months of the war's end, Washington took a leading role in bringing maximum international pressure on Moscow. Many analysts hold that the dispute provided one of the early manifestations of the Cold War. The Soviets finally pulled out in 1946 in return for a treaty pledge by Tehran that it would respect the status of the two 'socialist republics' of Azerbaijan and Kurdistan that the USSR had set up in northern Iran. But Washington gave all the assistance necessary to enable the Iranian armed forces under the pro-Western Iranian monarch, Mohammed Reza Shah Pahlavi, to crush those 'republics' within less than a year of the Soviet withdrawal.

Meanwhile, President Roosevelt remained ardent in his pursuit of close friendship with King Abdul Aziz. Their relations took a new turn towards military cooperation during the war, when the USA sought and expanded the Saudi Dhahran airbase for allied use. On his way back from Yalta, President Roosevelt met King Abdul Aziz in Egypt on February 14, 1945, and assured him of continued US support.[5] The two sides also discussed another important emerging issue, namely the plight of the Jews and their desire to return to the British Mandated Territory of Palestine – an issue which quickly developed into a major problem in US relations with the Arabs, but at the same time soon provided another significant niche for the USA in the region. These developments enabled a more systematic, elaborate and far-reaching American political, economic and strategic drive to penetrate a significant part of the Muslim domain in the post-Second World War era.

'Containment' and US Involvement in the Muslim World

After the Second World War, as the Soviet Union and USA emerged as the main global adversaries, Washington adopted a strategy designed to deter the Soviets from further expansion, on the one hand,

and to sap their energy and resources enough to cause the eventual collapse of Soviet power, on the other. Otherwise known as the Truman 'Doctrine of Containment', this strategy essentially aimed at defeating the Soviets by whatever means possible short of direct military confrontation. With Europe rapidly closing off as a theatre of confrontation for fear of a nuclear clash, Washington deemed it imperative to fill the power vacuum created by the collapse of the colonial order. It became assertive in all those areas of strategic and economic importance formerly within the realm of European colonialism and Japanese militarism. As such, a transformation link between colonialism and American globalism became an important issue that could not be lost easily when it came either to Washington's implementation of Containment or Soviet reaction to it. Indeed, only in this sense did Containment become relevant to US postwar policy treatment of the Muslim domain; and the USA also locked itself into position to compete with its European allies and oppose, not just communism, but any form of ideological and political behaviour – from revolutionary nationalism to non-aligned activism – that it saw as threatening US interests.

The USA launched its initial but most single-minded phase of Cold War imperialism, embarking on overt diplomatic and military interventionism in the domain of Islam as part of a wider game in Asia–Middle East. It did so within a four-dimensional approach.

First of all, it came down firmly on the side of anti-communist conservative elements, which in the aftermath of the Second World War came under increasing pressure from forces calling for radical restructuring of their societies and foreign policy orientations in pursuit of a more independent and equitable national existence. It made no difference to Washington whether the force was theocratic, autocratic or democratic; it embraced it as long as it was anti-communist and sided with the USA. It chose not to distinguish between local nationalism and international communism, adhered firmly to the belief that if 'they are not with us they are against us', and perceived every nationalist as a potential communist, to be treated no differently from a professed communist. Since the US–Soviet competition was seen as a zero-sum game, with any gain by one automatically a loss for the other, the retention and expansion of conservative forces and suppression of their radical counterparts became a central issue for Washington in its drive to become a global power.

Second, it resolved that the enemy must be confronted at all levels and in every major arena of human concern. Moral standards were subordinated to the realpolitik needs of American foreign policy, and human life and aspirations in areas of superpower competition became subordinate to US globalist interests. Political pragmatism and economic commercialism were combined in the USA's drive to penetrate not only the political structures, but also the economic base in many parts of the Muslim domain.

Third, it treated all communists as ideologically monolithic, and viewed all advocates of socialist transformation in the same light. No differences were recognized among them, or between them and radical nationalist reformers, who did not necessarily embrace Marxism–Leninism *per se*, but were inclined to use some of its elements for guiding their own social transformation and state-building.

Fourth, it decided that any method and any means, short of direct military confrontation with the Soviet Union and use of nuclear weapons, could legitimately be deployed to achieve its anti-Soviet goals. Thus, economic and military aid, cash distribution, bilateral and multilateral pacts were employed to maintain and strengthen receptive ruling elites and influential circles, to enable them to fight for their own and America's interests across the globe. Similarly, American aid, commercial organizations (in the case of the Middle East, oil companies) and intelligence agencies – most importantly the CIA – were given widespread government protection to carry out both overt and covert operations to promote US influence.

Within these parameters, the USA unleashed a series of operations across the Muslim domain. Although at the time the links in this chain could not easily be established, it can now, with the benefit of hindsight, be safely concluded that there was coordination between US policies toward the different parts of the domain. In the Muslim Middle East, Washington remained focused on Saudi Arabia, Iran and Turkey, and set out to use its penetration of these states as a base for wider anti-communist and anti-radical activities in the region. President Truman followed his predecessor's policy of maintaining close ties with King Saud, and continued to reassure him of long-term US support and protection. Finally in April 1950, in a secret agreement, the Truman Administration committed the USA to the defence of Saudi Arabia, alleviating its rulers' long-standing concern about perceived threats from the British-supported Hashemite Kingdoms of Jordan and Iraq. This was followed by upgrading the facilities of the Dhahran airbase, turning it into one of the most important strategic bases in the chain of regional commands America was seeking to build for containment of Soviet communism and for possible large scale future operations in the region. To all intents and purposes, Saudi Arabia was firmly placed within the US orbit on a long-term basis.

Meanwhile, the USA moved rapidly to strengthen its ties with the conservative forces, headed by Mohammed Reza Shah Pahlavi, in Iran. In fact, given his pro-Western upbringing and education, his growing fear of radical nationalism, supported by the pro-Soviet Iranian communist party, Tudeh, which swept Iran during the allied occupation and peaked just after the war, the Shah cooperated in transforming Iran from a non-aligned country to a close ally of the USA. When the war ended, the USA stepped up its military and economic aid to Iran. The American police and military advisory missions became more active than ever in reorganizing and equipping Iranian security and military forces. Although Millspaugh and his team had run into difficulties with many Iranian personnel, and by 1946 were forced to leave Iran, they were soon replaced by Max Thornburg, a former petroleum advisor to the State Department, and another group of American advisors, to help in planning the Iranian economy and eventually in drafting Iran's First Seven Year Development Plan (1949–55). Following the Shah's first visit to the USA, in 1949, Washington announced extension of the first Point IV (economic aid) program to Iran, and in the following year agreed to supply it with arms under the Mutual Defense Aid programme.

Washington's biggest opportunity came during Iran's oil national-ization crisis of 1951–53. The American oil companies had already launched a concerted drive to gain access to Iranian oil, with the growing support of Truman's Administration. In the meantime, the Iranian nationalist reformists, with a widespread popular following across the country, had become acutely hostile to the British hold on the Iranian oil industry. They resented the fact that Iran reaped very few financial and developmental benefits from its oil, that Britain excessively influenced Iran's national development and foreign policy priorities, and that this perpetuated major power rivalry in and over Iran, to the country's detriment.

Leading these Iranians within the National Front, a loose but nationwide coalition, was Dr Mohammed Mossadeq, a member of the landed aristocracy, but a consistent opponent of Pahlavi absolutism.

He had long been an advocate of democratic reforms, speedy social and economic development, and an end to foreign control of Iran's resources. He had endured many years of imprisonment under Reza Shah Pahlavi's rule (1925–41), and as a parliamentary deputy from Tehran had authored the anti-oil concession bill in 1944. The Shah, his conservative supporters and the British disliked Mossadeq, and his lack of Marxist–Leninist credentials made him distrusted by the Soviets. The Americans, however, remained ambivalent towards him at least until early 1953, quietly appreciating his anti-British stand, but finding his nationalist radicalism unsettling.

Nevertheless, given Mossadeq's surging popularity, the Majlis (Parliament) elected him prime minister in April 1951, leaving the Shah with no constitutional option but to appoint him to the position. After failing to secure a better oil deal from the British through negotiation, Mossadeq on May 1 declared the Anglo–Iranian Oil Company (AIOC), through which Britain controlled the Iranian oil industry, nationalized, and promised compensation. Mossadeq's action constituted the first act of nationalization in the Middle East; and could not have come at a worse time for London. Britain had recently lost what Lord Curzon called the 'British badge of its sovereignty in the Eastern hemisphere',[6] namely the Indian sub-continent, when India and Pakistan became independent in 1947; it was facing mounting postwar economic difficulties at home, and nationalist revolts in its Middle Eastern colonies and protectorates; and, at the same time, could not be confident of its partnership with Washington. It consequently rejected outright Mossadeq's national-ization, imposed an economic blockade on Iran, and resorted to gunboat diplomacy to force Mossadeq to back down. The interna-tional oil companies, most of them American, supported the British-initiated embargo on the purchase of Iranian oil. One reason was that they feared Mossadeq's nationalization might start a fashion in areas where they operated, another that they profited from the nationalization by increasing their production to fill the gap.

Mossadeq's refusal to retreat caused an unprecedented crisis in Anglo–Iranian relations. What drove Mossadeq was not just his feel-ing that he was morally right and that the Iranian people backed him, but the encouragement derived from the initial US endorsement of the nationalization as within Iran's sovereign rights, and the support that he received from Henry Grady, the outspokenly anti-British American ambassador in Tehran. Grady's attitude was also partly reflected by Secretary of State Dean Acheson, who subsequently wrote that the American 'interest lay in the threat that this controversy held for everyone's interests in the Near East...' and that in their approach the British were 'destructive and determined on a rule or ruin policy in Iran'.[7] Acheson sought as early as October 1952 to end the crisis with a solution involving American companies, but a dispute between the US Justice Department and the companies under US anti-trust laws frustrated his efforts. However, when the Eisenhower Administration took over in January 1953, the way was open for Washington to act.

President Dwight Eisenhower and, more importantly, his hardline anti-communist Secretary of State, John Foster Dulles, moved quickly to deal a final blow to Britain in Iran and indeed in the region. However, they could not do this without also getting rid of Mossadeq. His popularity by now was waning, largely due to growing economic hardship under the weight of the British blockade, which caused Iran's annual oil production to drop from 241.4 million barrels in 1950 to 10.6 million in 1952. The British argued that Mossadeq's leadership had thereby become vulnerable to a communist takeover because of his good working relationship with Tudeh, and that a viable alternative to it must be a government under the direct control of the Shah and his supporters. The USA accepted this argument; in one of its most successful covert operations the CIA, helped by British intelligence, engineered Mossadeq's overthrow in mid-August 1953 and brought back a somewhat reluctant Shah, who had fled to Rome a week earlier, to establish dictatorial rule with full US support. The key players in the operation were Allen Dulles, Director of the CIA (brother of the Secretary of State, and a shareholder in more than one American oil company); Loy Henderson, who had replaced Grady as American ambassador; and General Norman H. Schwarzkopf, formerly Commander of the New Jersey State Police, now a CIA operative attached as military specialist to the American Embassy in Tehran (and father of General Norman Schwarzkopf, who commanded the US-led alliance forces in the Gulf War against Iraq almost four decades later).

This operation was the first large-scale American intervention in the Middle East, and had far-reaching consequences. It confirmed Iran's position as an anti-communist frontline state and close ally of the USA. Further, it provided the USA with a centrally important strategic foothold on the Soviet border – a base from which to develop a strong anti-Soviet regional alliance. It also marked the end of the British monopoly over Iranian oil, and inflicted a serious blow to the British position in the region as a whole. The USA moved swiftly to resolve the nationalization crisis in a way conducive to the broadening of American economic and political influence in the region. In October 1953, John Foster Dulles commissioned Herbert Hoover Jr, a petroleum advisor and son of a former president, not only to find a solution to the dispute, but also to make sure that US companies acquired a share in the Iranian oil industry.

Hoover proposed an international consortium, theoretically to act as a customer of the National Iranian Oil Company (set up by Mossadeq in the wake of his Nationalization Act), but in practice to run the industry. The consortium was to be composed of British Petroleum, with a 40 per cent share; five American companies (Standard Oil of New Jersey, Standard Oil of California, Texaco, Mobil and Gulf), each with 8 per cent; the Anglo-Dutch Shell, with 14 per cent; and the French Compagnie Française des Petroles (CFP), with 6 per cent. Formation of this consortium, which became operational in November 1954, was a real coup for the American companies and yet another foundation stone in the overall structure for US dominance in the region. From then on, the Shah's dictatorship brutally suppressed all forms of dissent, and became structurally dependent on the USA for its survival and operations in the face of widespread domestic resentment and regional apprehensions. Iran became the largest recipient outside NATO of American economic and military aid, and political and cultural influence, and was promoted as a key client to protect American interests in the region.

Meanwhile, another dimension was added to US involvement in the Middle East: it stemmed from US support for the creation of Israel and its subsequent adoption of the Jewish state as a strategic ally. Undoubtedly, President Truman's motives in committing the USA to support Israel from the start, in the face of opposition from Arabs and Secretary of State George Marshall, who favoured UN trusteeship of Palestine, and strongly advised against recognition of a Jewish state there, for fear of creating an enduring bloody conflict, have inspired much controversy over the years. Whatever the points of contention, President Truman was motivated more by humanitarian and domestic rather than long-term strategic considerations. After a period of indecisiveness, the President decided in favour of recognizing Israel, for three important reasons. First, King Abdul Aziz had let him know that while he was opposed to the creation of Israel, he would not allow this to affect his friendship with Washington. The second was his personal concern about the plight of the Jewish people in the wake of the Holocaust, as well as pressure from the Jewish lobby both directly and indirectly through Democrat leaders who kept urging him to accord recognition in order to secure the Jewish vote in the Presidential election due later in 1948. The third was a fear that the Soviet Union might recognize Israel and then gain a foothold in the Middle East by sending troops under Article 51 of the UN Charter to fend off possible Arab aggression against it. After the UN backed the partition of Palestine into a Jewish state and an Arab state, the USA recognized Israel within hours of its proclamation on May 14, 1948 – an act which replaced the Jewish problem and Diaspora with a Palestinian one, and set off one of the most tragic, bloody and complex conflicts in the modern history of the Middle East.

It was obvious from the start that a Jewish state could not survive on its own in the heart of the Arab world; and this would give the USA, though in some ways unintentionally, another significant strategic foothold in the region. By the late 1950s, as the politics of the region and the Cold War evolved, the USA found it imperative to adopt Israel as a strategic ally, and an important leverage and connecting point in America's attempt to check radical Arab nationalist challenges and Soviet activities in a region that it now valued very much for both its oil riches and geostrategic importance, but feared for its volatility and unpredictability.

Meanwhile, the US penetration of Iran and Saudi Arabia did not take place in isolation from American activities in other parts of the Muslim domain. It came on the heels of important developments in South Asia and the Far East, and found connection to America's reaction to these developments. The end of British colonial rule of the Indian subcontinent in 1947, and the new geopolitical realities that this created, provided another power cavity for the USA to seek to fill in South Asia. The subcontinent broke up into two independent entities: the Islamic state of Pakistan and the predominantly Hindu but secular state of India, whose ensuing hostilities rapidly pulled them into opposing foreign policy objectives and orientations. As India under Prime Minister Jawaharlal Nehru assumed the mantle of the true inheritor of British rule, and sought to chart out a non-aligned foreign policy which would play down its colonial past and raise its credentials as an independent democratic state in its own right, Pakistan could not alleviate its initial fear of India as an awesome threat to its survival. Given this, and the need to tap a common chord between its four main national groups, Pakistan's anglophile founding father, Mohammed Ali Jinnah, decided that Pakistan should have an Islamic identity, but with a secular Westminster democratic system of government.

Initially, the USA did not favour partition of the subcontinent; some in Washington considered Pakistan's creation 'a mistake'[8] and not conducive to post-British regional stability. Following the partition, Washington worked hard to court the Nehru leadership in the hope of luring India into an anti-Soviet friendship. In early October 1949, President Truman invited Nehru on an official visit to the USA, where he was given a hero's welcome and reminded that the USA shared with India common goals of independence, freedom and democracy, and was therefore willing to provide whatever assistance it could. However, Nehru could not be moved from his determination to steer India on a foreign policy course of geopolitical neutrality, with friendly relations with all powers, including the Soviet Union.

Nehru's message of neutralism in the American–Soviet rivalry caused considerable discomfort to many in Washington, even though the Soviets had at first shunned Nehru's government as bourgeois and called for a communist revolution against it – something which led in 1949 to New Delhi's arrest of some 100,000 Indian communists and their sympathizers.

The communist victory in China, the Korean War, in which the USA took the lead to enforce its policy of containment, and the Japanese Peace Treaty, tilted the picture further against any prospects for close Indo-American friendship, and in favour of an American–Pakistan alliance. This development also subsequently pressured Nehru to lean gradually towards the Soviet Union.

Like the unprovoked Japanese attack at Pearl Harbor, the Chinese and Korean episodes brought the worst out of the USA, by helping to fuel anti-communist hysteria there. Although McCarthyism had very complex roots, this development played an important role in inaugurating its nasty phase by the early 1950s, firmly and enduringly placing the conduct of American foreign policy under the control of Cold War 'hardliners', who already acknowledged no alternative to the strengthening of American power and globalism as the means to combat communism. The episodes also served as a litmus test for the USA to decide who were its friends and enemies. Those who failed to support the USA unequivocally in the fight against communism were viewed, irrespective of their reasoning and rationale, as either communists or communist sympathizers. Washington became more assertive than ever in its determination to build a US-backed regional security belt, supported by a second line of defence, from Japan to Australasia to the Middle East, as part of a global system of containment.

While swiftly confirming Japan's postwar status as a full ally, and under US security protection within the framework of a peace treaty and security pact signed on September 8, 1951 in San Francisco, the USA attracted widespread criticism from not only China and the Soviet Union, but also India, which viewed the whole development as part of an aggressive American design for global hegemony. In the same year, the USA concluded several other bilateral and multilateral security treaties. The most important of the bilateral treaties were with South Korea, with the Philippines, which as a former American colony was now feeling vulnerable, and Taiwan, to where the Chinese nationalist government had fled, while claiming still to represent all of China. Washington also concluded with two of its loyal, predominantly Anglo-Saxon supporters, Australia and New Zealand, a multilateral security pact that became known as the ANZUS Treaty.

As India continued to develop good relations with the Soviet Union, recognized communist China, refused to send troops to Korea, despite New Delhi's initial support for the UN resolution authorizing the use of force against North Korea, and criticized the Japanese Peace Treaty, the US could no longer court India for close ties. It also found irritating India's persistent efforts to promote non-alignment in world politics – something that led to the founding of the Non-Aligned Movement in 1955, which the USA regarded as furnishing a smokescreen for communist infiltration of the Third World. As a consequence, the USA rapidly turned away from India to embrace India's arch enemy, the Islamic state of Pakistan. While unperturbed by Pakistan's declared Islamic identity and remaining confident of Jinnah's pledge that Pakistan would have a secular democratic setup, the USA welcomed its strong support of the American position on Korea with a contribution of 5,000 troops, of the Japanese Peace Treaty, and of assurances that its Islamic ideology would provide no fertile ground for communism. This soon led to the conclusion of various economic and military agreements, locking Pakistan into the American orbit.

Meanwhile, the USA moved swiftly to reap benefits from Ataturk's pro-Western secularist legacy in Turkey, and exploit its traditional anti-Russian posture and postwar fear of Soviet communism. While encouraging suppression of local communists, Washington rapidly extended to Turkey, as it did at the same time to Iran and Pakistan, large amounts of American economic and military aid. Ankara even went a step further than Iran, Pakistan and Saudi Arabia to accommodate American bases, enabling it to claim a special status for its relationship with the USA.

Under the Eisenhower Administration from 1953, the USA set out on an urgent mission to sponsor a system of regional security alliances, stretching from West Asia to Southeast Asia. In February 1953, President Eisenhower professed a definite need for such alliances against what he called the 'enemies who are plotting our destruction'.[9] At first, the USA almost simultaneously signed bilateral economic and military agreements with Iran, Pakistan and Turkey, then encouraged them to sign agreements among themselves as a prelude to entering regional alliances as part of the US strategy to develop a global alliance for containing Soviet, and now also Chinese, communism. John Foster Dulles believed these countries shared a common enemy in communism, and could not only defend themselves with American support but also prevent the spread of communism to a number of Arab countries, south of the Euphrates and across to Egypt. Initially the USA also wanted Afghanistan to join such alliances, but Kabul was unwilling to antagonize its northern superpower neighbour, the Soviet Union, with which it shared a long border and extensive crossborder ethnic ties. Kabul also had a simmering border dispute with Pakistan, inherited from British India, and was not prepared to forego its claims in order to enter into an alliance with Pakistan.

The result was the conclusion of two important regional pacts. One was the Baghdad Pact, comprising Iran, Iraq, Turkey and Pakistan. Although the USA never formally joined this Pact, it was formed with US support in October 1955 and was renamed the Central Treaty Organization (CENTO) in 1958, after the overthrow of the pro-British Iraqi monarchy by a nationalist coup led to Iraq's withdrawal. Another was the South-East Asia Collective Defense Treaty (SEATO), forged in September 1954. Like CENTO, SEATO was supposed to be a defensive alliance, of Thailand, the Philippines, Pakistan, USA, United Kingdom, France, Australia and New Zealand. India, Burma, Ceylon and Indonesia were also invited to join, but they declined. These alliances were to complement the USA's bigger prize, the North Atlantic Treaty Organization (NATO), which had been established in 1949 – a development which the Soviets countered by setting up the rival Warsaw Pact after West Germany's admission to NATO in 1955. With Turkey a member of both NATO and CENTO, and Pakistan a member of CENTO and SEATO, two Muslim countries, although with varying outlooks, became key elements in an American chain of global alliances against the Soviet Union and its communist allies. The only Muslim countries left out of the American orbit were Afghanistan and those Arab states which fell to radical Arab nationalism following the Egyptian coup of 1952, and which now became a source of concern for not only diehard French and British colonialists, and Israel, but also the USA – an issue which will be discussed shortly.

By the mid-1950s, the USA had achieved a position of eminence in most of the key states in the Muslim domain. Its influence in Saudi Arabia, Iran, Pakistan and Turkey could not be underestimated, and its inroads into pro-Western monarchical Jordan and Morocco (independent from 1956) appeared substantial. As we shall see later, this was soon to be supplemented after the Suez War of 1956 by a US strategic partnership with Israel in the wake of the rising influence of Nasserism and its friendly ties with the Soviet Union, and the perceived threat this posed to American interests in the region.

The USA was able, more than a decade later, to use this foundation to press for the development of a US-sponsored triangular relationship between Iran, Saudi Arabia and Israel, upon which it could solidly rest long-term American dominance. It fell within what became known as the Guam or Nixon Doctrine, and in the wake of the British withdrawal from the Persian Gulf by 1971 as part of an overall pullout from East of Suez due to financial difficulties. The Nixon Doctrine, formulated in the light of America's Vietnam fiasco, postulated that from then on the USA would support a number of select allies and provide them whatever non-combat support, short of nuclear weapons, they needed to safeguard not only their own interests but also those of the United States in different parts of the world. In the predominantly Muslim Persian Gulf–West Asian region, it selected the Shah's Iran to be this ally, within what it called a two-pillar approach, with Iran the senior and Saudi Arabia the junior pillar. Given the close security relationship that had developed between the Shah's regime and Israel, Washington appeared to consider this approach most appropriate for achieving what by then had emerged as its three main interrelated goals: opposition to Soviet communism, ensuring uninterrupted oil supplies from the Middle East, and safeguarding Israel's survival and strategic edge over the Arabs. Of course, in this instance neither the Nixon Doctrine nor its twin pillar approach worked, because the Americans underestimated the depth of historical differences between Iran and Saudi Arabia, and between them and Israel, and failed to perceive that the Shah's regime was built on sand. It nonetheless gave a clear indication of the direction in which Washington wanted to shift the region.

During the period of US power consolidation in the Muslim domain in the 1950s, there was not a single credible Islamic challenge. Islamic forces in the domain as a whole appeared allied with secular or semi-secular authorities, or controlled by them. If there were religious agitations here and there, they were quickly suppressed and posed little political threat to either the USA or its client regimes. The three challenges – one serious and two less so – came mainly from secularist sources: radical Arab nationalism, and Indonesian and Afghan non-aligned nationalism.

Nationalist Challenges

The Arab nationalist challenge was articulated by the new revolutionary pan-Arabist republican regime of Gamal Abdul Nasser, which seized power through a coup from the British-client monarchy of King Farouq in Cairo in July 1952. Nasser was unique among the Arab leaders of his generation. He was a Muslim, but with a secularist, revolutionary domestic and foreign policy posture. He essentially sought what many of his fellow Egyptian and Arab nationalists, including some Islamists, had longed for: to transform Egypt into a modern, independent state, and unite and radicalize the Arabs as one people against what he called all forms of feudalism, colonialism, imperialism and Zionism, as well as pro-Western Arab conservatism. He was initially keen to promote democracy at home and non-alignment in foreign policy. However, he underestimated the hostility that he would encounter immediately from Israel and European powers (especially the British and French) and subsequently from the USA, and their allies in the Arab world, and overestimated the support he would receive from the Soviet Union, whose interest in the Middle East was essentially embedded in a desire to exploit Nasser's revolutionary radicalism and the Arab–Israeli conflict to enhance its own bargaining position against the USA. He also could not fully grasp how far the USA was prepared to go to protect Israel and maintain its oil-rich Iranian and Arab clients.

As he consolidated power, he ultimately could not establish more than another secular authoritarian regime, nor achieve more than lopsided modernization at home and fragmented results in foreign policy. His domestic policies resulted in an Arab socialist system, which had all the weaknesses of a closed, command based political and economic order. His foreign policy, while partly successful – especially in relation to nationalizing the Suez Canal and turning the Anglo–French–Israeli attack on Egypt in 1956 into a political victory, that made him an Arab hero almost overnight – divided the Arab world into radical nationalist or Nasserite and pro-Western conservative camps. It also acutely alienated the USA, which could accommodate neither Nasser's brand of radical Arab nationalism nor his tilt towards the Soviet Union from 1955. In fact, it was this factor which led Washington to withdraw its offer of World Bank funds for building Nasser's most important domestic project, the Aswan High Dam – a development which in turn prompted Nasser to nationalize the Suez Canal.

Even so, Washington tried to avoid driving Nasser and his supporters deep into Soviet arms. During the Suez war it strongly condemned Israel and its British and French allies for invading Egypt, and concurred with the Soviet Union for the first time during the Cold War in demanding their withdrawal. However, for Nasser the die had been cast; he could no longer trust the West, including the USA. As after the Suez war he leaned more towards the Soviet Union for support – a move to which Moscow responded by withdrawing its recognition of Israel, supporting the Palestinian and Arab cause, and providing generous economic and military aid – the USA turned its back on Egypt.

In a chain of action and reaction, Nasser forged even closer ties with the Soviet Union, not only as Egypt's arms supplier, but now also financier of the Aswan Dam. Under the Eisenhower Doctrine,

Washington set out to contain Nasser's radical nationalism by identifying it with 'international communism' and supporting anti-Nasserite forces wherever possible in the region. In 1958, the USA launched its first overt military operation in Lebanon at the request of Lebanon's pro-Western Christian President Camille Chamoun, who claimed to perceive a serious threat from radical Arab nationalism, as embodied by Nasserism. A major confrontation between the American and Nasserite forces was avoided only when Chamoun's term of office expired, and when Washington and Cairo reached an understanding that it was not then in either's best interest to allow the situation to escalate into a regional confrontation.

Nasser's foreign policy also did little to advance the Palestinian cause, contain Israel's growing power, or limit US support for Israel and America's expanding role in the region. Israel's defeat of Egypt, Jordan and Syria in the 1967 Six-Day War resulted in the loss of Sinai, the Golan Heights, Gaza, the West Bank and, most inflammatory of all, East Jerusalem, a huge humiliation from which neither Nasser nor the Arab world could easily recover. The more Israel triumphed militarily and expanded territorially, while the Arabs remained divided, the more Nasser and his supporters, including all the Palestinian organizations he nurtured – most importantly at first Fateh, then the Palestine Liberation Organization (PLO) under Yasser Arafat, faced hopelessness, frustration, and increased Arab vulnerability to the USA, as a power capable of determining peace and war and influencing the course of Arab destiny. By the late 1960s, Nasser had realized the need to come to terms with the USA, but died in 1970 before he could take any lasting steps in that direction.

The task was left to his successor, Anwar al-Sadat (1970–81), who 'de-Nasserized' Egypt and downgraded Egypt's ties with the Soviet Union, seeking peace with Israel and friendship with the USA. After the October 1973 War with Israel opened the way for diplomacy, Sadat made peace with Israel by concluding the Camp David Agreements of 1978 under US auspices, at the price of putting Arab nationalism on the backburner and leaving the Palestinians, the Syrians and their Arab supporters to fend for themselves. Thus, Egypt too at last succumbed to US prowess. Sadat lost his life in the process; he was assassinated by his radical Islamist opponents in October 1981, but his successor, Husni Mubarak, pursued his legacy to cement Egypt's position as a faithful US ally.

This dramatically enhanced US regional dominance, and strengthened Israel's position to the point that it was able to launch a war on Lebanon in 1982 with full impunity, in an attempt to destroy the PLO and put an end once and for all to the Palestinian problem. Although the PLO and Palestinian cause survived, the major outcome of all these developments was growing disillusionment among many Islamists and radical nationalists not only in Egypt, but also across the Arab and Muslim world, an issue which is discussed in detail in the next chapter.

Another challenge, though not as serious as that mounted by radical Arab nationalism, stemmed from Indonesian nationalism, under the secularist Sukarno. As a Dutch colony subjected to Japanese militarism, multi-ethnic but predominantly Muslim Indonesia proclaimed its independence in 1945, although it took three years of bloody struggle before the Dutch acknowledged it in 1949. In the first three years of independence, Indonesia experienced relative stability under conservative governments, but the favourable circumstances ended by 1952 when Muslim Reformists and traditionalists split into two separate parties and the PKI, the pro-Chinese Indonesian communist party, grew in stature and influence, ushering in a period of bitter inter-party politics. The elections of 1955 worsened the situation: they ended parliamentary democracy, dashing the hopes of new groups of securing a meaningful share in power. As political instability settled in, the army two years later assumed wider administrative powers, and the PKI expanded its influence – a development which was also aided by the Sukarno regime's 'confrontation' with newly independent (from 1957) British-supported Malaysia. This led Sukarno in 1959 to abrogate the provisional constitution, inaugurate what he called Guided Democracy, and resort to governance on the basis of an alliance between himself, the army and PKI. Amid growing economic difficulties and foreign policy disputes over Malaysia and New Guinea, he also swung fairly sharply towards the communist camp by buying arms from the Soviet Union and seeking close relations with China.

The Western powers, most importantly the USA, grew rapidly apprehensive about Sukarno, whose nationalism, and refusal to endorse the US stand against communism and join the US-sponsored SEATO, found no legitimacy in American strategic thinking. The USA sought to counter Sukarno's perceived menace in two ways.

One was to provide secret military assistance to the rival PRRI (Pemerintah Revolsusioner Republik Indonesia) government at Bukittingi. On May 18, 1958, 'US pilot Alan Pope [was] shot down over Ambon while secretly helping PRRI rebels'[10] – a development which infuriated the Sukarno leadership. Another was to promote in Indonesia, as in Southeast Asia as a whole, the virtues and benefits of the 'American way of life', 'expressed through the activities of the Peace Corps and the Agency for International Development'.[11] It has also been suggested that the US ambassador in Jakarta actively cultivated Sukarno's opponents, especially in the military, and that the group of officers who pushed Sukarno from power after suppressing the attempted leftist coup of 1965 had ties with the Americans, although this has not been conclusively established.

Whatever the actual US role in fomenting an anti-Sukarno backlash, his successor, General Suharto, readily welcomed a major role for US and other Western economic interests and influences, and rapidly shifted Indonesia's foreign policy in a pro-USA direction.

Afghan nationalism was of a different kind, but perceived by Washington as a less important challenge than those of the Arabs and Indonesians. As a traditionally non-aligned, ethno-tribal, poor Muslim state, with a potentially serious border dispute with Pakistan, Afghanistan had never gained much significance in the American geostrategic calculus. As pointed out earlier, Afghanistan wished to avoid involvement in the US–Soviet rivalry for fear of antagonizing its powerful northern neighbour, the Soviet Union, and foregoing its border dispute with Pakistan. But at the same time its authoritarian rulers, especially Prime Minister Mohammed Daoud (1953–63), the rival cousin and brother-in-law of King Zahir Shah (1933–73), who subsequently toppled the king in 1973 and declared Afghanistan a republic, wanted to modernize Afghanistan in response to postwar pressures and to the challenges arising from the border dispute with Pakistan. Having no interest in Marxism–Leninism *per se*, and seeking friendship with a distant power, Daoud first approached Washington in 1954 for economic and military assistance and for help in resolving the Afghan–Pakistan dispute. But Washington's refusal, on the grounds that Afghanistan was not strategically and economically attractive, and that Pakistan was more important to US interests, prompted Daoud to turn to the Soviet Union. The post-Stalin Soviet leadership under Nikita Khrushchev, which viewed Afghanistan favourably due to its refusal to join western-sponsored alliances, welcomed Daoud's request and initiated a substantial programme of economic and military assistance. It also backed Afghanistan in its dispute with Pakistan, seeing close friendship with Afghanistan as a means of propagating its newly proclaimed policy of peaceful coexistence and non-interference in internal affairs, and countering America's growing containment strategy in the region.

By the early 1960s, Afghan–Soviet relations had reached a point where the Afghan armed forces, the only organized agent of change in the country, had become mostly Soviet-trained and equipped. Hundreds of Soviet-trained young Afghans (some, such as the future Soviet-installed communist president of Afghanistan, Babrak Karmal, recruited by the KGB) and Soviet advisors assumed important positions in running the Afghan military, economy and administration. The danger of this soon became evident to both the Afghan and American leaderships. Kabul sought means to play off the two powers, and the USA sought to counter Soviet influence by offering Afghanistan economic aid. However, what it offered was too little too late. While US economic aid from 1955 to 1979 amounted to about $532 million, and declined rapidly from the late 1960s because of US preoccupation with the Vietnam war, Soviet economic and military aid, on more favourable terms, came to over $2.5 billion during the same period.[12] Although Daoud stepped down as prime minister in 1963, mainly over the dispute with Pakistan, the King's 'experiment with democracy' in the next decade faced the usual difficulty of how to modernize a traditional and socially divided society. The King's lack of experience and political decisiveness, as well as his determination to block Daoud from regaining power, created sufficient dislocation for Daoud to stage a comeback through a largely bloodless military coup in July 1973. This time he did so with the help of the Parcham (Banner) faction of the tiny informal Afghan communist party (the People's Democratic Party of Afghanistan – PDPA), that had come into existence in the mid-1960s as a result of the Soviets' growing influence in Afghanistan. Daoud declared Afghanistan a republic, with close neighbourly relations with the Soviet Union, but a major border dispute with Pakistan. This initial alliance with the communists radicalized Afghan Islamists of Muslim Brotherhood persuasion under a group of theologians who had received training in Egypt's oldest Islamic institution, Al-Azhar, and since the early 1960s had formed the Jamiat-i Islami (Islamic society) at Kabul University to counter the growth of Soviet influence.

Some of the leading figures of this group later became leaders of the major Mujahideen groups against the Soviet occupation of Afghanistan in the 1980s.

At first Daoud moved against the Islamists, but once he had consolidated power, as a nationalist, he also wanted to reduce his dependence on communists and vulnerability to the Soviet Union. To this end, he sought to improve ties with Pakistan and to solicit aid from some of the Soviet Union's staunch regional adversaries, such as President Sadat of Egypt and the Shah of Iran, and Moscow ceased to trust him. In 1976, he informed Washington of the danger posed by communists in Afghanistan and sought American help, but to no avail. He was advised to talk to the Shah, America's regional policeman under the Nixon Doctrine. But the Shah's own position was by now very precarious; he would soon be confronted with a revolution which would overthrow him and transform Iran into an anti-American Islamic republic.

Daoud's political naiveté and autocratic behaviour, as well as his inability to gain sufficient support from the USA to change Afghanistan's domestic and foreign policy orientation, played an important role in enabling the Soviets and their Afghan surrogates to carry out the bloody coup of April 1978, declaring Afghanistan a Democratic Republic, with fraternal ties with the Soviet Union. Given the highly fractured nature of the PDPA, its members' lack of experience and historical legitimacy, and Stalinist behaviour, as well as President Hafizullah Amin's decision to flirt with the Americans in the face of growing insurgency in the country, this opened the way for the Soviet invasion of Afghanistan 20 months later, inaugurating a tragic phase of bloodshed and ideological extremism in the evolution of Afghan politics.

By and large, only moderate Islam had historically prevailed in Afghanistan, but now as the circumstances changed, a variety of Islam, ranging from moderate to radical, was deployed as ideology to mount a credible resistance to Soviet occupation, and this was done with full US support. Thus Afghan nationalism, unlike that of Arabs and Indonesians, and Washington's inability or unwillingness to understand the needs of Afghanistan, led Afghanistan in a direction that came to haunt the USA 23 years later, as detailed in the next chapter.

The containment strategy locked the USA into a very narrow mindset. It limited its options to a policy of penetrating and coopting whichever country it deemed necessary. It also encouraged intolerance, intimidation and intervention towards those who disagreed with its international position. It made the promotion of alternative strategies replete with political cost at home and loss of face abroad. The USA spared no efforts to back, promote and even impose regimes in the domain of Islam which were thoroughly corrupt and contrary to all the democratic and liberal values in defence of which the USA claimed to act. It paid little or no attention to the suffering and aspirations of the peoples living under such regimes, and upheld its stand on human rights very selectively and only in relation to its adversaries, not in respect of those it wished to subordinate. Washington repeatedly ignored what its policy behaviour was supporting in Saudi Arabia, Iran, Pakistan and Indonesia or for that matter many other Muslim countries. Only very occasionally, and even then under intense pressure, did it find it necessary to cajole a friendly regime towards reform, as in the case of Iran in the early 1960s, but without going the distance necessary to ensure the success of the reforms. Its opposition to radical nationalist forces, through fear of their becoming susceptible to Soviet communism or a conduit for anti-American subversion whether in the Arab world or elsewhere in the Muslim domain, proved very costly in the long run, depriving the USA of the opportunity to develop a firm understanding of what these forces were all about, and to come to terms with them as embodying the aspirations of peoples who had suffered greatly from and under European colonialism.

Successive American administrations, from Truman to Nixon, could not see how in the Muslim world their policy actions, together with the failure of secularist and semi-secularist forces and the clash between traditionalism and modernism in the context of postwar pressures, could open the necessary space for many Muslims to turn to their religion, with which they had been imbued for 14 centuries, as an ideology of salvation, resistance and reform. The USA's post-1945 preoccupation with the three goals of defeating Soviet communism, controlling oil and other significant natural resources in the Muslim world, and protecting Israel despite its inherently expansionist and discriminatory nature as a confessional state, led it to become too self-indulgent and self-righteous and disinclined to develop strategies which could win peoples' minds and hearts in the domain of Islam. They certainly achieved a great deal of success in all the three goals, despite even the 'OPEC revolution' of the early 1970s which enabled producing states to wrest the power of supply and pricing of their oil to a considerable extent from the Western oil companies. They appeared to equate America's power over many ruling elites with influence over their peoples. But this was not really the case, as the events of subsequent decades came to prove.

4

The Great Issues

In recent times, three major issues have proved instrumental in reinforcing the cumulative effect of European colonization and the USA's postwar global penetration of the Muslim realm. They have created the conditions for sharpening the enmities between the two sides, shaping their perceptions of one another, and motivating the West, and more specifically the USA, to seek to marginalize political Islam in world politics. The first was Iran's mass revolution of 1978–79, which overthrew one of America's key allies, Iran's absolute ruler Mohammed Reza Shah, replaced him with a decidedly anti-American Islamic regime and shaped the USA's perception of radical Islam. The second was, and is, the Palestinian problem, which has profoundly affected Muslim views of the USA, seen as unable or unwilling to rein in Israel and promote resolution of the problem. The third is the Afghanistan conflict: here the contradictory US approach contributed greatly to creating an environment in Afghanistan that led to the tragic events of September 11, 2001.

The Iranian Revolution*

As discussed in the previous chapter, the Shah acted as a bridgehead for US influence in Iran and the wider region from 1953, when the CIA reinstalled him to rule in support of US global interests. This development encumbered the Shah with an indignity from which he could never recover, and rapidly led to Iran's political, economic, military and foreign policy dependence on the USA. The CIA's role delegitimized the Shah's rule in the eyes of many Iranians, and made it the subject of criticism by the Soviets and radical Arab nationalists. These linkages made his regime vulnerable to US dictates, to the extent that it could never achieve a proper symmetry in its relations with Washington. As the Shah consolidated his dictatorship with full US support, he had little or no choice but to pursue two contradictory goals. One was to maintain his position as undisputed ruler, presiding over a monarchy that had been the nominal bastion of power for some 2,500 years, and defined very much by traditions rather than innovations. Another was to adopt a set of national development and foreign policy priorities and objectives which would please the USA and maintain his credentials as its most trusted ally in the region. The first goal required constant centralization of power, while the second necessitated decentralization of politics, allowing a free enterprise mode of social and economic change to take hold. In short, he had to operate in two opposite directions: one underpinning his own position, the other geared to match Iran's interests with those of his patron power.

This set the parameters within which the Shah could operate in both domestic and foreign policy arenas. If he acted outside them, he risked complicating his relations with his external source of security and increasing the fragility of his situation at home. Yet it was also clear from the start, to both the Shah and Washington, that he could not in the long run rely on coercion alone to maintain his rule. In fact, by 1959, after he had consolidated his power, the Shah publicly acknowledged this, and the Americans prodded him towards reform to expand his power base and gain popular legitimacy.

In the early 1960s, the Shah inaugurated a reform programme, which he called the 'White Revolution' or 'the Revolution of the Shah and the people', involving 'no bloodshed' and 'no class struggle'. The 'White Revolution' called for land reform, improvement in education, health and agriculture, and female emancipation. But it was essentially designed to open up new sources of public support for the Shah's regime in rural areas and among youth and educated women, and dissipate the oppositional energy of thousands of unemployed high school and university graduates by sending them to do military service in rural areas. It was also in relation to this programme that the Shah was made acutely aware of the leverage the USA held on him. When he showed some reluctance to proceed with the reforms in the way the Americans wanted, Washington reacted firmly. In 1961, the Kennedy Administration imposed on him its choice of prime minister in the person of Ali Amini, Iran's ambassador to the USA and a friend of the Kennedys – a development which prompted the Shah to do everything possible not to lose his pole position with the USA. While initially accepting Amini, he made life so unbearable for him that within two years of appointment, and after successfully launching the land reform programme, Amini resigned, enabling the Shah to take over the reform programme. His reforms produced mixed results. They certainly helped to divert many urban youths from oppositional activities and gave hope to a small number of educated women in the main cities, especially Tehran. However, on the whole they proved superficial, were seriously undermined by an inefficient and corrupt ruling elite and bureaucracy, and brought little or no change in the Shah's relationship of dependence on the USA.

A similar fate awaited the Shah's bolder attempts at the turn of the 1970s to popularize his regime and adjust his relations with the USA. He began by moving to play a more assertive role in the politics of the Organization of Petroleum Exporting Countries (OPEC), which in favourable international conditions was gaining strength, giving OPEC members more control over their oil supplies and pricing. He felt that if he achieved a determinant role in OPEC politics, he would become not only financially independent, empowered to undertake a more aggressive phase of Iran's modernization, and to buy international friends in support of a bigger regional role for Iran, but could also transform his dependent relationship with the USA to one of (somewhat asymmetrical) interdependence. But he was unable to score much in this respect. His OPEC successes quadrupled Iran's oil income from $4.1 billion in 1973 to over $17 billion in 1974[1] – a development which whetted his appetite for accelerated social and economic progress, and military modernization of Iran, as a precondition for transforming it into what he called 'the world's fifth economic and military power' by 1985. But all he could institute was a modernization process along the lines of 'Americanization', with the USA very strongly placed to recycle Iran's newly found oil wealth by supplying most of its modernization requirements and guiding his changes with some 37,000 highly paid US experts employed in all fields of activities in Iran by 1978.

Meanwhile, the USA had the option of using the other pillar of its Gulf policy, namely Saudi Arabia – then the largest oil producer within OPEC, and therefore most influential within the organization's politics – to pull the Shah back should he deviate too far from the American line. For example, in 1975 the Shah was redoubling his efforts to achieve regional superpower status and provide leadership to the Third World's demand for restructuring of the international political and economic order. Saudi Arabia used its position as OPEC's largest producer to stem any increase in Iran's oil income by supporting a freeze in oil prices, leaving the Shah desperate for funds to finance his development plans and meet people's expectations. This meant that he could not alter his dependent relationship with the USA, and the best he could hope for was to transform Iran into a dependent regional power. As his poorly planned and badly implemented modernization programme caused massive social and economic dislocation, the contrast between his regime's oil wealth and dependence on the USA simply highlighted the basic contradictions underlying his rule. He could neither achieve modernization nor surmount the indignity of being seen as an American puppet. If anything, Iran's interests were further interlocked with those of the USA by the Nixon Doctrine, under which the USA would supply Iran with whatever military hardware the Shah wanted, short of nuclear weapons.

The consequences of this were severe, as I noted more than two decades ago:

> The overall result was that Iran in the 1970s became more dependent on the United States, and thus more open to American political, economic and social [and military] influence than ever before, though the nature of this dependence was different from that in the past. Particularly in view of a fast-growing number of Americans with influential positions in the Iranian administration, economy, armed forces, and social services, many Iranians became increasingly convinced that the Shah was essentially an American puppet, who had sold their country to the United States. They felt that their cultural identity, traditional beliefs, and values as well as traditional yearning for freedom and justice were being seriously threatened, and that their natural resources were being exploited to benefit foreigners more than Iranians.... They felt that the country had been led in a direction... not of their own choosing, and that was contrary to their needs and expectations. They could not help but implicate the United States continuously in what the Shah was imposing on them.[2]

Washington was well positioned to realize the Shah's circumstances and foresee the storms which were gathering to wash away one of its critical allies. CIA field officers had alerted their superiors to the Shah's growing difficulties. President Carter, who took office in January 1977, had applied pressure on the Shah, as part of an overall drive to make human rights a major issue in US foreign policy, to move towards political reforms. The Shah had consequently begun a limited and very slow process of political liberalization, that by 1978 had enabled a number of opposition groups, hitherto underground, to make their presence felt on the political scene. This process played an important role in opening cracks in the Shah's rule – cracks which he could not close, encouraging people to question the nature of his dictatorship and where it was taking Iran. Here was a clear vindication of Alexis de Tocqueville's warning that the most dangerous moment for an autocracy is when it begins to liberalize.

However, right to the very end, Washington could not recognize or grasp the enormity of the Shah's problems and the depth of the Iranian people's resentment towards the USA as his backer. President Jimmy Carter continued to view him as the USA's most trusted and enduring regional ally. The Shah and his associates persuaded Carter and many of his key advisors that 'His Majesty was in full control of the situation' and there was no cause for alarm. Even as two underground militant groups, Fedayeen-i Khalq (People's Sacrificers) and Mujahideen-i Khalq (People's Fighters), stepped up their activities, including targeted assassination of Westerners, especially Americans, the Carter Administration apparently accepted the Shah's dismissive description of them as isolated Marxist and Islamic-Marxist groups respectively, in no way indicative of popular attitudes towards his regime. It continued to meet the Shah's economic and military requests, despite increasing criticism from Congress. Under the US–Iranian agreement of August 1976, commercial trade between them was to rise from $10 billion in 1974–76 to $40 billion during 1976–80; and their military trade, about $10 billion in 1973–76, was to total another $15 billion in 1976–80.[3] As late as November 1978, while Iranian students were demonstrating outside the White House against the visiting Shah, Carter praised him as a 'strong leader', and declared, 'we look upon Iran as a very stabilizing force in the world at large'.[4]

The key policy makers in Washington failed to discern that the Shah and his policies had alienated a wide range of citizens. His autocratic rule alienated all those who wanted a democratic Iran. His modernization, which put heavy emphasis on high-technology, import-substituting economic growth and military acquisitions but far less on improvement in the social sector, caused much dislocation and disillusionment for ordinary Iranians, who could neither cope with the pace of change nor understand where it was taking them, while his pro-American secularism progressively put Iran's influential Shi'ite Islamic establishment offside. This establishment had played a significant role since the sixteenth century in relations between state and society in Iran. Prior to the advent of the Shah's father, the Shi'ite clerics had had a prominent role, under a four-centuries' old understanding with the state, confirmed in the 1906 Constitution, in overseeing the state's functioning, to ensure that it did not deviate from the main path of Shi'ite Islam. Relations between the Shia establishment and the political authorities were always prone to tensions and conflicts, but rarely to the extent that transpired under the Pahlavis. The constant efforts of its two Shahs to undermine the clerics' power, and thus neutralize a potential source of major opposition to their rule, led to a sharp deterioration in relations. Some clerics had staged a major uprising against Reza Shah in the mid-1930s, and continued their oppositional activities against his son, denouncing in 1953 his CIA-backed usurpation of power as illegitimate.

One of the most active figures was Ayatollah Ruhollah Khomeini (1902–89), who rose from a relatively poor background to become a well-trained theologian. Gifted in both oratory and public relations through religious networks, he steadily grew more intolerant of the Pahlavi dynasty and determined to use Islam as a political ideology to organize public resistance. After backing a teachers' strike in 1960–61 for better pay and working conditions, he stepped into the limelight in 1963 with a forceful sermon in which he castigated the Shah, the USA and Israel almost in equal terms and advocated a religious uprising. The Shah's notorious secret police, SAVAK, which had been set up with CIA and FBI assistance, and had developed close links with its Israeli counterpart, Mossad, arrested Khomeini, but he was soon released for fear of a religious backlash. However, he continued his agitation, and in 1964 denounced the Shah's granting of extraterritorial rights to the USA. He was banished to Turkey, from where he moved to Iraq, to teach and preach among the Iraqi Shi'ites for the next 14 years.

The years of exile deprived Khomeini of a direct presence on the Iranian political scene, but could not prevent him from maintaining his criticisms of the regime from abroad. He was able to do this in the context of the ongoing political-ideological rivalries and, at times, open border conflict between the Shah's regime and that of the Iraqi strong man Saddam Hussein, and through contacts with his peers and followers in the Iranian city of Qom, the Shi'ites' centre of spiritual power and learning, and in the network of mosques throughout Iran. When the revolution against the Shah's rule broke out in 1978, Khomeini and his radical Islamist followers were ready to play a critical role. Although the revolution started as an anti-Shah phenomenon, led by the Shah's political opponents in pursuit of democratic reforms, what distinguished Khomeini from other revolutionary leaders and his peers was the simplicity of his messages, appeals and promises. He, first among his peers, abandoned the traditional critical but relatively quiescent clerical line to argue that the Shi'ite establishment's function was no longer to oversee the working of the government but rather to run it. This, together with his Islamic messages that freedom from the Shah's tyranny was a religious duty and necessary for the spiritual and social well-being of Iranians, won over not only many young radical clerics, but also thousands of ordinary citizens. The latter could not understand the complex ideological language of the Shah's political opponents, but could easily comprehend Khomeini's messages. By late 1978, when the revolution had involved every segment of Iran's population, including some upper and middle class supporters of the Shah who had benefited from his policies but no longer found his rule conducive to a comfortable existence, Khomeini and his cleric supporters were able to seize the leadership of the revolution.

The USA appeared poorly informed, shocked, paralysed by events, incapable of understanding the nature of the revolution, the depth and breadth of opposition to the Shah's rule, the strength of the hold Shia Islam had maintained on the Iranian people, or the way that Khomeini and his radical supporters utilized this hold to give the revolution an Islamic direction. The Carter Administration failed to establish any meaningful contact with the opposition: it could neither assist the democratic elements within it, nor open a dialogue with the Khomeini headed elite to reassure it that the Administration understood its position. It simply continued to hope that the Shah could hold on by making some democratic reforms. Not until December 9, 1978 did President Carter finally express doubt about the Shah's chances of survival, with a remark that boosted the opposition, led Khomeini to close all doors to any compromise solution, and left the

Shah with little choice but to flee. He appointed a new prime minister, Shahpur Bakhtiar, from the ranks of his secular opponents, and departed Iran on January 17, 1979, ostensibly only for a short stay abroad. Khomeini, who had gone to France after Saddam Hussein, under pressure from the Shah, expelled him from Iraq six months earlier, returned to Tehran shortly thereafter to a tumultuous popular welcome. Bakhtiar's government faced collapse, with many of the Shah's generals switching to the opposition, and Khomeini subsequently declared Iran an Islamic republic. He ended the 2500 year-old Iranian monarchy, advocated the rights of the Mostaz'afin (weak, disinherited) against the Mostakberin (oppressors), denounced the Shah's past policies and the US support for him, and vowed to export Iran's revolution to the region against what he called 'US-backed' 'satanic' regimes.

Khomeini's anti-American Shi'ite Islamic regime initially focused on a *jihadi* approach to reorganizing and reshaping Iran's domestic and foreign policy priorities and objectives, with the aim of Islamizing politics and society according to Khomeini's interpretation of what constituted a Shi'ite Islamic state. Khomeini soon endorsed and assumed the position of *Vilayat-i Faqih* (guardianship of the jurist or supreme spiritual and political leader). This amounted to establishment of a theocracy, with individual rights and freedoms and societal processes subordinated to the leadership's ideological and political need. It led to a period of severe political repression and turbulence. In a bloody confrontation, Khomeini's activists, led by his closest confidant and shrewdest strategist, Ayatollah Beheshti, sought to weed out political and ideological opponents. They included not only Fedayeen-i Khalq and Mujahideen-i Khalq, but also such Islamists as Abdul Hassan Bani Sadr, Iran's first Islamic President. A self-styled Islamic economist, who had taught in France for many years, Bani Sadr was initially favoured by Khomeini as an adopted son; and this was important for his popular election to the presidency from the start of 1980. But his inexperience in the cut-throat revolutionary politics of Iran, and his opposition to acts of Islamic militancy and to the growing ascendancy of Beheshti and his operatives, soon put him at odds with Khomeini's determination to construct an Islamic system and protect it against internal and external enemies. The latter most notably included the USA and its regional allies as well as secularist regimes, such as that of Saddam Hussein in Iraq, which viewed Iran's Islamism as a threat. In the confrontation between Khomeini's zealots and their opponents, hundreds of people were killed, including

Beheshti and a number of Khomeini's confidants. While Bani Sadr managed to flee to France, many opposition leaders were arrested or forced into exile, and Khomeini's activists achieved full political ascendancy.

The Khomeini regime was by no means widely emulated by the rest of the mainly Sunni dominated Muslim countries. It nonetheless in many ways reflected the aspirations of Muslims in the region and beyond who had felt humiliated and frustrated by their bitter experiences with the West. It inspired and emboldened many political forces of Islam from both sides of the Sunni–Shi'ite sectarian divide to challenge the influence of the West in the Middle East and elsewhere in the Muslim world. These forces were inspired as never before to seek either a peaceful or a revolutionary political and social transformation of their societies along Islamic lines, free of Western hegemonic influences.

What drastically changed the picture were two further developments. One was the hostage crisis, resulting from Khomeini's Islamic militants' seizure of some 50 American diplomats for 20 months from November 4, 1979. Although Khomeini did not publicly back the hostage taking, he expressed understanding and sympathy for the militants' action. He appeared content to exploit the episode to humiliate the USA for supporting what he saw as the Shah's 'crimes' against the people; to maintain public support by fostering perpetual anti-American rage; to divert public attention from what soon emerged as the revolution's failure to fulfil its promises of delivering democracy and a better standard of living; and to demonstrate his capacity as a strong and decisive leader. As the crisis dragged on, the USA found itself helpless. Its only military rescue mission, in mid-1980, ended in fiasco in an Iranian desert, making further attempts impossible. The USA had to endure an unprecedented period of pain and degradation, despite its status as a superpower.

The other development occurred in Lebanon, as a result of Iran's sponsorship of the Lebanese revolutionary Shi'ite group Hezbullah (Party of God). Founded in 1982, it was very much modelled on the Iranian Hezbullah. This had become active following the Iranian revolution, intended to serve Khomeini's leadership and give the revolution an Islamic direction, but soon fragmented into various paramilitary and intelligence units and committees, serving as watchdogs and foot-soldiers of the clerically dominated Islamic Republican Party (established in 1979 and dissolved in 1987, when

Khomeini deemed the existence of parties inadmissible in an Islamic polity). The Iranian Hezbullahis, who had been in contact with Lebanese Shi'ites even before the Iranian revolution, were largely responsible for organizing, training and financing the Lebanese Hezbullah. They were enabled to do so by favourable conditions in Lebanon. Inspired by Khomeini's successes, the Lebanese Shi'ites had become very susceptible to radicalization, for two main reasons. One was the failure of Lebanon's consociational democratic arrangements to give them the greater share in the power structure to which their rapid growth in numbers since the census of 1932 entitled them. Another was the suffering inflicted by Israel's invasion of Lebanon in 1982. These factors, together with Khomeini's regime's eagerness to give weight to its call for a region-wide revolution and its stand against Israel and the USA (a stand which also enticed the Syrian government into supporting the Iranian initiative), enabled Iran to play a key role in Hezbullah's emergence as a formidable force.

When the Reagan Administration decided to provide a face-saving device for the Israelis to end their costly operations in Lebanon by dispatching American marines there as peacekeepers, Hezbullah was ready for bloody action. It launched a number of attacks in 1983–84 on the US embassy and US and French barracks in Beirut, killing hundreds of foreigners, including 241 US marines. Although Washington immediately withdrew its forces, Hezbullah continued its operations, not only successfully targeting Israeli troops and their Christian allies in Israel's self-declared security zone in southern Lebanon, but also seizing American and European hostages to strengthen its bargaining position and that of Iran. While hostage-taking ended by the turn of the 1990s as Iran's priorities were changed by its needs to achieve broader acceptance in international politics, Hezbullah's operations against Israel continued, generating much popularity for it in Lebanon and the region as the first credible Arab Islamic 'liberation front'. It refined its guerrilla tactics to the extent that Israel finally decided to cut its losses and make a unilateral withdrawal from southern Lebanon in 2000, delivering Hezbullah its biggest victory. Its successes acted as a catalyst for radical Palestinian Islamist groups, galvanizing them to walk down the same path against Israel – an issue which will be discussed later.

It was essentially Khomeini's and Khomeini-inspired *jihadi* Islamism that led Washington to develop a particular mindset about radical political Islam, and perceive and react to it more through its own bitter experiences with Khomeini's regime than anything else. It immediately labelled as 'fundamentalist' all political forces of Islam that challenged or refused to recognize the USA's hegemonic interests and accord it status as a global power. Washington considered these forces an anomaly and a menace in the international system, therefore to be globally isolated and suppressed. Hence its deployment of 'Islamic fundamentalism' as a pejorative term to discredit them as irrational, irresponsible and extremist forces, dedicated actually or potentially to international terrorism. In this, it was backed by a number of pro-Israeli scholars, analysts and popular columnists, such as Bernard Lewis and Daniel Pipes. Washington felt no imperative to go beyond this impulsive understanding to explore what historical and contemporary conditions engendered the Khomeini phenomenon, and how those conditions could be wisely and judiciously addressed in political, economic and cultural terms to prevent the phenomenon within and beyond Iran inspiring radicalism in the wider domain of Islam. It simply adopted the old approach of containment and power balancing, placing Iran under strict political, economic and military sanctions, as the best way to break the back of Iranian Islamism and those associated with it from outside. In this context, Washington even turned to one of the region's most unsavoury regimes, that of the Iraqi dictator Saddam Hussein, to achieve its objectives.

As pointed out earlier, Saddam Hussein and many of his Arab counterparts had felt challenged by Khomeini's Islamic universalism. However, whereas his counterparts were covered by the USA (and lacked the resources and any tangible excuse to respond), Saddam Hussein was in a different position. He felt that while Khomeini's regime was in post-revolutionary turmoil and subject to American sanctions, he had an opportunity to attack Iran in order not only to secure favourable resolution of a border dispute with it over the Shatt al-Arab, but also to bring down Khomeini's regime, thereby furthering his own ambition to become the hegemon of the region. Iraq's military offensive, starting in September 1980 and supported by most of the Arab states against the common perceived Iranian threat, began the longest, bloodiest and costliest war in the Middle East's modern history. Iran was able to defend itself, but only at very heavy human, economic and social cost. The war lasted until mid-1988 when finally Khomeini, under the threat of unravelling the Iranian revolution, accepted a UN proposal for a ceasefire. Although publicly the USA declared its neutrality, and called on both sides to disengage, it was soon courting Saddam Hussein as a potential ally and Arab bulwark against Khomeini's regime.

The Republican Administration of President Ronald Reagan (1981–89) was happy to provide Iraq with satellite photographs of Iran's military positions and troop movements, to tolerate the sale by various US companies of high-technology products which could be used for military purposes, and to encourage its allies to sell sophisticated weapons systems to Iraq. The USA also supplied some 30 per cent of Iraq's agricultural needs, virtually all 'under US government credit and subsidy programs that eventually totalled $1 billion a year'.[5] In mid-April 1990, a US Congressional delegation, headed by senior Republican Senator Robert Dole, visited Baghdad to convey a special message from Reagan's former Vice President, President George Bush, to Saddam Hussein, to assure him of the US desire for even better relations.[6]

Of course, all this came to a crashing halt when Saddam Hussein's forces invaded a fellow oil-rich Arab state, Kuwait, on August 2, 1990. The USA and Israel were by then worried about Saddam Hussein's production of weapons of mass destruction, especially chemical and biological arms. The Iraqi invasion came at a critical time for the USA. The Soviet Union was on the verge of collapse, and no longer able to defy the USA by supporting an old friend such as Saddam Hussein. The USA wanted, as President Bush put it, to kick the 'Vietnam syndrome' and establish its position as the world's only superpower. It could not let the invasion stand, and the unpredictable Saddam Hussein to gain control over Kuwaiti oil and threaten the flow of Saudi oil and therefore the USA's interests. As the USA led an international coalition in 'Operation Desert Storm', mainly from Saudi Arabia, to reverse the invasion, Iran declared its neutrality. Even so, after achieving its goal by the end of February 1991 (although without taking out Saddam Hussein's regime, for fear Iraq might disintegrate and that Iran might benefit from this because of its sectarian ties with the Iraqi Shi'ite majority population), Washington put Iran in the same basket as Iraq. It now treated both as 'enemies', against whom it vowed to protect its 'friends', that is the oil-rich members of the Gulf Cooperation Council (GCC),[7] formed in the early 1980s for defence against Iran.

The Democratic Administration of Bill Clinton (1993–2001) devised the policy of 'dual containment' to punish Iran and Iraq equally. The policy was devised by one of President Clinton's key advisors on the Middle East, Martin Indyk, formerly a well known pro-Israeli Jewish activist likely to reflect Israel's concerns as much as the USA's in formulation of the policy. Clinton sought to enforce this policy even by promulgating extra-territorial laws in 1995 to bar any foreign company from investing more than $40 million in the Iranian gas and oil industry. This was despite the fact that a strong wind of change had come to blow across the Iranian political landscape – a development which had been in the making for some time, well before Khomeini's death in mid-1989.

In its early years, the Khomeini Islamic regime undoubtedly evolved in many ways as the mirror image of that of the Shah. It adopted an Islamic constitution, and created an electoral process of political legitimation and citizen participation in politics. But it failed to establish an inclusive political order which could allow Iran to be defined as any more than a theocratic state or be treated as such by those outside forces which found its behaviour threatening to their interests. It grew as exclusive and intolerant of opposition as the Shah's regime had been. This, together with the Islamic regime's inability to fulfil its promises of good government and a better life for most Iranians, engendered the risk that any future structural political change might be as violent as the one which brought the regime to power. The regime remained vulnerable to spontaneous popular uprisings of the kind which initially opened the way for destruction of the Shah's rule.[8]

This, however, does not tell the full story. It explains only the Islamic *jihadi*[9] (or 'resistant and exertive') dimension of Khomeini's leadership. This dimension involved ideological and policy behaviour that could enable the regime, first of all, to integrate politics with religion, consolidate its own position and thereby achieve a Shi'ite Islamic transformation under hostile circumstances. Its emphasis was naturally mainly on resistance, defence and reassertion in securing the revolution to bolster the regime, and enabling it to deflect internal and external forces which actively opposed it or perceived it as threatening.

However, once this objective had been achieved, by the mid-1980s, another related dimension in Khomeini's leadership was waiting to emerge at an opportune time. This was the *ijtihadi*[10] (or 'creatively interpretive') dimension, which had been working in tandem with the *jihadi* dimension, but had been overshadowed by it because of the conditions prevailing in the Islamic regime's early years. In the tradition of Iranian Shi'ism, Khomeini had been regarded as a *Mujtahid* (creative interpreter of Islam) long before the revolution, given his emphasis on the need for a creative interpretation of Shi'ite Islam and its application in accordance with changing conditions and the course of history.

In other words, Khomeini had never believed in Islam being frozen in time; he had upheld it as a religion for all times, peoples and conditions. This was evident not only in the series of lectures he delivered in Iraq in the early 1970s, subsequently published under the title *Islamic Government*, but also in numerous *fatwas* or religious rulings that he issued, before the revolution against the Shah's regime and its US ally, and after the revolution to establish a very complex but nonetheless modern Islamic governmental system. While founding this system on Islam and resting final religious-based temporal authority in the hands of the *Vilayati Faqih*, he ensured that it was participatory, with the public involved in the processes of political legitimation, policy formulation and implementation. Hence his notion of popular elections, and a popularly-elected president.

This generated a generic division within the ruling clerics, giving rise to two main factions. One was the *jihadis*, who upheld a somewhat 'combative' interpretation of Shi'ite Islam, and became popularly known as 'conservatives' or 'hardliners'. Under the conditions of post-revolutionary internal strife and the eight-year long war against Iraq (1980–88), this group initially achieved political ascendancy, gaining control over most of the instrumentalities of state power. Another group, the *ijtihadis*, or those who adopted a more liberal interpretation of Shi'ite Islam, were given the title of 'pragmatists' or 'moderates'. While alive, Khomeini was regarded as a leading *jihadi* and *ijtihadi*, with paramount constitutional and revolutionary powers to establish some kind of balance between his dual factional followers.

Khomeini's death in June 1989 changed the situation. While the approach of the *ijtihadi* faction was at least partly reflected in the policy behaviour of President Hashemi Rafsanjani (1989–97), who played a major role in securing the release of several Western hostages and ending hostage taking in Lebanon, the *jihadi* faction was patronized by Khomeini's successor as *Vilayati Faqih*, Ayatollah Ali Khamenei. The Iran–Iraq war had enabled the *jihadis* to divert people's attention from the revolution's original promises of democratic freedoms and higher living standards, and from Iran's deepening economic and social problems, its persistent international isolation, and the rapid growth of the post-revolutionary youth to dominate the electorate. But after the war ended in a stalemate, the scene was set for sharpening of the *jihadi–ijtihadi* division in Iranian politics. Nonetheless, Rafsanjani managed to keep a lid on the situation by cooperating closely with Khamenei and refraining from stepping too much outside the ideological parameters set by the *jihadis*.

However, this situation could not endure for too long. It was clear that the parameters of the ideological framework had to be widened, as the clerics gained confidence in power, to accommodate a faster process of *ijtihadi* reform in pursuit of the revolution's original goals. By the early 1990s, one prominent clerical thinker and activist, Abdulkarim Soroush, had already placed the issue of expansion of ideological parameters on the agenda.[11] His argument about Islam's compatibility with democracy and its flexibility as a religion to be applied in time-space under changing conditions had already provided wider legitimacy to the position of the *ijtihadis* in their debate with the *jihadis*. What boosted this shift further was the fact that despite the *jihadis'* dominance in the state power structure, the electoral process was robust and inclusive enough to produce the main catalyst.

Against this backdrop Mohammed Khatami rose from the ranks of the *ijtihadis* to be elected President of Iran in a landslide in July 1997. This is not to claim that he is not a *jihadi* in defence of Iran and Islam whenever necessary, but clearly his platform from the beginning was *ijtihadi* in character. It underlined a firm conviction that the time had come for Iran to exit rapidly from a political culture of *jihad* to that of *ijtihad* if it were to meet the changing conditions in Iran and the international environment. To realize this objective, Khatami called for the intertwined goal of achieving 'Islamic civil society' as a precondition for and in tandem with 'Islamic democracy', and of rationalizing Iran's foreign relations, based on the principles of 'dialogue' between civilizations and cross-cultural understandings within the international system of nation-states.[12] In essence, he called for a new Shi'ite Islamic vision in accordance with the changing times and conditions – a vision which Khatami claims Khomeini would share if he were alive.[13]

While treating Iran's Islamic constitution as sacrosanct, he has stressed not only that Islam enshrines its own concepts of civil society and democracy, but also that the constitution is committed to promoting such concepts as a means to serve the common good. He has emphasized that these concepts, although different in their roots from their Western counterparts, are not necessarily in 'conflict and contradiction in all their manifestations and consequences' with those arising from Western traditions of rationalism and liberalism. He claims that '[t]his is exactly why we should never be oblivious to the judicious acquisition of the positive accomplishments of Western society.'[14]

Khatami states that in an Islamic civil society, 'although it is centred around the axis of Islamic thinking and culture, personal or group dictatorship or even the tyranny of the majority and elimination of the minority has no place; ... man ... is venerated and revered and his rights respected; ... and citizens enjoy the right to determine their own destiny, supervise the governance and hold the government accountable. The government in such a society is the servant of the people and not their master, and in every eventuality is accountable to the people whom God has entitled to determine their own destiny.' He stresses that an Islamic civil society is not one 'where only Muslims are entitled to rights and are considered citizens. Rather, all individuals are entitled to rights, within the framework of law and order.' To Khatami 'respect for human rights and compliance with their relevant norms and standards is ... the natural consequence of ... [Islamic] teachings and precepts.' Furthermore, he makes it clear that an Islamic civil society 'seeks neither to dominate others nor to submit to domination', but at the same time, 'as instructed by the Holy Qur'an, considers itself entitled to acquire all requisite means for material and technical progress and authority.'[15]

He places a high premium on the notion of freedom as central to constructing and operating a stable and vibrant Islamic civil society, although he stresses that in practice freedom, whether at individual or societal level, cannot be limitless. 'We want a system based on abstinence and high morality that only comes through relentless endeavour and the courage to embark upon moral and spiritual growth. This is true freedom, but people need to be taught to see it this way.'[16] He considers the importance of freedom of thought and expression and diversity of views as central to substantiation of an Islamic civil society. He quotes Khomeini who argued that, '[i]n Islamic government there should always be room for revision. Our revolutionary system demands that various, even opposing, viewpoints be allowed to surface.'[17] He notes, 'we must achieve a new vision and understanding. Relying on current religious leadership is necessary but not sufficient.'[18]

Khatami condemns censorship and the banning of opposition as a solution to Iran's problems. He shuns those who seek to impose 'their rigid thinking on Islam and call it God's religion [because] they lack the intellectual power to confront their opposite side's thinking on its own terms', and thus 'resort to fanaticism.'[19] He argues for plurality of views and freedom to express them as a condition for developing an Islamic civil society. He states, 'we cannot expect any positive transformations anywhere unless the yearning for freedom is fulfilled. That is the freedom to think and the security to express new thinking.'[20] '[T]ransformation and progress require thought, and thought only flourishes in an atmosphere of freedom. But our history has not allowed human character to grow and to be appreciated, and thus the basic human yearning for thinking and freedom has been unattended at best and negated at worst.'[21]

Khatami's concept of Islamic civil society is thus more conditioned on moral than material standards. While involving a measured degree of separation of politics and capital, political and social pluralism, freedom of thinking and expression, and government intervention in public life to help the needy, and to ensure justice and the implementation of Islamic-based laws, it ultimately relies on moral force to win the day. Like many other religious-political thinkers, Khatami is keen to emphasize that moral, virtuous and humane existence delivers a better standard of living in economic and social terms.

This belief also strongly shapes Khatami's international outlook. He stresses the importance of peaceful coexistence and mutual respect, and the need for dialogue of civilizations among peoples and states in world politics. Ever since coming to power, he has persistently underlined the need to promote the common humanity that can bond peoples together in peace rather than the earthly differences that lead them to conflict. He has sought to apply this approach to Iran's relations with not only its 'arch enemy', the USA, but also Iran's traditional regional rivals, such as Saudi Arabia.

Of course, Khatami's reform agenda has not had a smooth run in either the domestic or foreign policy arena. On the domestic front he has been seriously challenged by those *jihadi* who have been unable or unwilling to make a quick leap into his *ijtihadi* culture. These have used their domination of the judiciary, the security and armed forces, and numerous decision-making councils and committees, and their close association with the *Vilayati Faqih*, to frustrate some of Khatami's civil society reforms as extra-*ijtihadi*, extra-constitutional and pro-Western. They have also rejected some of Khatami's proposed dialogue of civilizations and cross-cultural understanding for broader and better foreign relations, including a possible rapprochement with the USA, as undermining the strength of Islam and pleasing the West and Western-dominated forces of globalization. They have argued that Khatami's reforms in general are bound to unravel the fabric of the revolutionary Islamic Iran that Khomeini bequeathed, and to provide opportunities for the West, especially the USA, to restore its influence in Iran. As the reform process has moved forward, the *jihadis* have increasingly targeted one of the issues at the heart of the process, namely freedom of thinking and expression. They have used their control of the judiciary and law enforcement agencies to seek to thwart the process.

Khatami's response has been to use his public mandate judiciously in dealing with his *jihadi* opponents. He has acted within the framework of the constitution not only to pursue a peaceful and orderly *ijtihadi* course of change, but also to educate his opponents to behave similarly, and repeatedly condemned extra-legal means as a substitute for non-violent debate and behaviour. Although his reforms have not been altogether free of violent confrontations, such as the July 1999 and subsequent student demonstrations, which attracted disproportionate use of force by the *jihadis*, on the whole his methods of peaceful dialogue and conciliation have proved fairly credible, though at one important price, that he has managed his reforms only within a strategy of 'two steps forward, one step back', inevitably slowing the pace of reform to the dismay of some of his supporters.

Even at this pace, he still maintains majority public support, and has succeeded in converting a number of leading *jihadi* clerics to *ijtihadis*. These include Ayatollah Khalkhali (known as the 'hanging judge' in the revolution's early days), Abdullah Nouri, and the leaders of the student militants who, in November 1979, held American diplomats in Tehran hostage for 15 months: they are all now firmly lined up behind his reforms.[22] Whatever Khatami's difficulties so far, he scored a stunning electoral victory in May 2001 for a second term, following a similar victory by his supporters in the February 2000 *Majlis* (National Assembly) elections. This would now make it harder than ever for his opponents to reverse his course of reform.

Khatami has undoubtedly put Iran on a somewhat indigenous course of civil and democratic change that manifests a number of elements at the very least fulfilling the criteria for what the West would consider a minimalist model of democracy. However, success will ultimately depend on maintaining the process of reform within the Islamic framework, avoiding the risk of its evolving beyond that framework after Khatami's presidency ends. Khatami's ability to bridge the gap between *jihadis* and *ijtihadis* without seriously compromising the process itself, and to improve Iran's economic conditions, which seriously trouble many of those who voted him into office, will also be crucial.

The US attitude towards Iran will be another factor. Late in the second term of his presidency and after the dismal failure of 'dual containment', which came under heavy criticism from such influential figures as two former National Security Advisors, Zbigniew Brzezinski and Brent Scowcroft,[23] President Clinton finally took note of the changes in Iranian politics. He and his Secretary of State, Madeleine Albright, made a number of overtures in response to Khatami's call for dialogue and exchanges between the American and Iranian peoples. Washington lifted the ban on some Iranian exports, and hoped for a road map to be worked out for eventual government-to-government contacts. On a number of occasions US officials, including Dr Albright, came face to face with their Iranian counterparts during UN-sponsored talks in 1999–2001 over the Afghanistan conflict. These, together with increased informal cultural and economic exchanges, raised expectations of a breakthrough.

However, substantial progress was impeded by hardliners on both sides. A number of members of the US Congress, some of them staunch supporters of Israel, argued against rapprochement, citing Iran's opposition to the Middle East peace process, support for Hezbullah, alleged efforts to acquire weapons of mass destruction, and the continuing presence of hardliners in Iran's power structure. On the other side, Iranian *jihadis* argued against compromising the principles of the Iranian revolution and Khomeini's legacy by reestablishing formal relations with the USA. They argued that the USA continued to treat Iran as a 'rogue' state, and had done little tangible either to release Iranian assets frozen in the USA following the hostage crisis, or to end the sanctions against Iran it imposed and kept reinforcing following the revolution. The issue was left to Clinton's Republican successor, President George W. Bush.

Unfortunately, President Bush assumed power with a manifestly hostile position towards countries such as Iran, and made no effort to pick up where Clinton had left off. His combative approach to asserting America's role as the only global power quickly proved alarming to the USA's adversaries. Although initially he was relieved at Iran's acquiescence in the US 'war against terrorism' following the September 11 events, by December 2001, when the USA had succeeded in dislodging the Taliban and Al Qaeda from power in Afghanistan, his Administration changed tack. It accused Iran of providing sanctuary to fleeing Taliban and Al Qaeda leaders and of causing problems for Hamid Karzai's new government in Kabul. This completely ignored the record of Khatami's government. It had all along opposed the Taliban and Pakistan's sponsorship of it, had played a positive role in helping the various Afghan groups to reach agreement at the Bonn conference on a government to replace the Taliban, then declared its full support for Karzai's interim government, and promised $560 million in aid for reconstruction of Afghanistan.

During a visit to Tehran in January 2002, UN Secretary-General Kofi Annan praised Iran's conduct in relation to Afghanistan. However, this did not prevent President Bush branding Iran in his State of the Union address in late January 2002 as a member of an 'axis of evil' together with Iraq and North Korea. President Bush and his advisors have displayed little understanding of the complexity of the Iranian system, where power and politics are structured such that when it comes to confronting external pressure and threat, no distinct division can exist between the ruling radical and moderate factions, and the latter have little room to manoeuvre but must join forces with their radical political opponents. By all indications, President Bush's approach has had two kinds of effect. On the one hand, it has somewhat rattled the Iranian hardliners, whom he has branded as an 'unelected few' imposing their will on the Iranian people; this may have prompted them to hand over, in June 2002, 16 Saudi members of Al Qaeda to Saudi Arabia, in the knowledge that this would please Washington.[24] On the other, it has played right into the hands of the hardliners by strengthening their position in the Iranian power set-up. Ayatollah Khamenei has not only barred all contacts by Iranian officials with the USA, but also condemned the Bush Administration's policy behaviour and what he has termed 'arrogance of power', and called on the Iranian people to fight any form of US interference in Iran's internal affairs. And President Khatami has echoed and endorsed these sentiments.

The Palestinian Problem

The second issue, which originated before the first, arose from Western, and more importantly US, support of the Jewish state of Israel. Initially the Western powers and the Soviet Union may have been driven more by moral and humanitarian than realpolitik considerations – given the historical European persecution of the Jews and the abominations of the Holocaust – to legitimize the creation of Israel in 1948 out of the predominantly Arab-populated Palestine. But the subsequent Western approach to the enduring Palestinian problem and Arab–Israeli conflict has been largely driven by realpolitik motives. The US embrace of Israel as a strategic partner within a decade of its creation, matched by a commitment to guarantee its security irrespective of its effect on the Palestinians in particular and the Arab–Muslim world in general, has been a misjudgement of gigantic proportions. It may have been beneficial to domestic and Cold War politics, but only at the cost of tension and turbulence in America's relations with the Muslim world. Washington's massive financial and military assistance to enable Israel to maintain a strategic edge over its Arab neighbours, and its political protection of Israel at the UN and in other international forums, could only perturb the Arab masses, and generate the basis for anti-American resentment among Muslim peoples in and beyond the region.

The turning point came with Israel's victory in the 1967 war, which enabled it not only to occupy more land, but also to capture and then annex East Jerusalem, to form with West Jerusalem the 'united capital of Israel for ever'. This caused huge anguish in the Muslim world's relations with the West. If the domain of Islam had until then remained somewhat aloof from the Arab–Israeli conflict, it now had a legitimate reason to be involved not only in support of the right of Palestinians to an independent state of their own, but also in pursuit of freeing the Muslims' third most holy place from Israeli occupation. Many Muslims regarded Israel's annexation of East Jerusalem as an assault by Jews on Islam and an affront to Islam's doctrinal treatment of Jews as followers of a respected religion, and were aghast at the thought of Muslims being humbled by non-Muslims taking over their holy site. They felt a sense of humiliation similar to that they suffered at the hands of the Crusaders and European colonialists. They were equally pained by Washington's tepid reaction to Israel's occupation and the West's general sympathy for Israel, believing that it was the Zionists who committed the first sin by taking over Palestinian land and establishing the state of Israel on it.[25] They began seriously to question America's attitude towards the Arabs and Muslims in moral, philosophical and political terms.

Israel appears to be a fully fledged democratic state, with a highly institutionalized, legal-rational and pluralist political order, robust civil society, high level of social and economic development and standard of living, and an impressive level of industrial-military capacity (including weapons of mass destruction, especially nuclear). What disturbed Muslim intellectuals and activists most was what the USA persistently overlooked about Israel. They pointed to the fact that Israel was established, and endured, as much as a confessional entity as a secular and democratic state, heavily influenced by Judaism, which served as the foundation of state legitimacy and identity, rendering its system less participatory than that of a liberal democracy. It was, and is, in some ways exclusive, with the state focused on catering more for its Jewish citizens than its non-Jewish (mostly Arab) inhabitants. The result has been an underlying tension that has characterized the development of the Israeli state since its inception, and has at times erupted into open conflict, affecting state cohesion and functions.

Many Muslims also stressed that Israel's political and territorial strength has not exactly been domestically resourced. It has developed rather as a rentier state, depending heavily on outside, specifically American, assistance. For example, from 1949 to 2002 US grants to Israel totalled over $87 billion,[26] and from 1991 the annual amount registered a dramatic rise, reaching a little more than $4 billion in the fiscal year of 2000.[27] Of the total amount, more than $41.5 billion was in military grants and over $29 billion in economic grants. This was in addition to the $2–3 billion that private Jewish sources in the USA donated annually over many years. Altogether US aid – from both official and private sources – has come to account for about 10–15 per cent of Israel's annual income. This, plus other benefits that it reaps from its strategic alliance with the USA, has proved critical to Israel's ability to maintain its domestic order and at the same time acquire social, economic and military resources[28] on a scale that has enabled it to emerge as a strong actor in the region.

It is further intimated that Israel exists as a confessionally/ territorially/security-driven actor in a region to which it has little or no organic links, and has developed as an implanted European piece of real estate. This has intertwined Israel's sovereignty with Judaism and with a need for a certain amount of territorial expansion as an important imperative for enforcing the viability of the Israeli state. This, in turn, has impelled it to live in a state of perpetual insecurity and isolation. Thus, the task of protecting and asserting its sovereignty against those whose territories it has occupied and whose enmity it has invited – the Palestinians and some of Israel's Arab neighbours – has produced a powerful nexus between Israel's conditional democratic order and foreign policy behaviour. No matter what its legal-constitutional arrangements and constraints, democratic values and practices, and norms of civil society, to maintain its position as a viable state, Israel has necessarily had to bear the brunt of being an expansionist power. In Muslim eyes, it has proved an assertive and, if required, aggressive actor, as it has been on numerous occasions (especially in its 1982 and 1996 invasions of Lebanon), and an occupier since 1967 of even those territories which were left for Palestinians after the creation of Israel: Israel is the only occupier of its kind in the world, in violation of UN resolutions and international law.

Further, Muslims hold that the USA has persistently overlooked that it sides with a state that has been progressively taken over by Jewish extremists. Initially, Israel came into being with a promise of democratic moderation, but since the early 1970s has experienced a rapid increase in religious extremist politics. Various parties and groups have succeeded in exerting far greater political influence than their size would normally allow, and have done so by exploiting Israel's conflict with the Palestinians and its other Arab neighbours. This has induced some potentially dangerous shifts in Israeli politics. Not only has political assassination found its way into Israel's political life, as with the gunning down of Prime Minister Yitzhak Rabin in November 1995, but Israel has also become more and more vulnerable to extremist postures. The election of rightwing Israeli prime ministers, Benjamin Netanyahu (1996–98) and Ariel Sharon (2001–) essentially represent the growing power of the Israeli Right, dedicated to the triple goals of 'Greater Israel', suppression of the Palestinian resistance by whatever means, and humiliation of Arabs. This has weakened the forces of political centrism, and made Israel's politics more volatile, driving it towards more religious-driven nationalistic aggressive policy behaviour. These aspects of Israel, and Washington's benign attitude towards them, have cumulatively helped galvanize Muslim activists against Israel, and led them to become distrustful and resentful of the United States. Many of them view the US–Israeli alliance as a Jewish–Christian conspiracy and a gross injustice, ensuring perpetuation of the Palestinian problem and Arab–Israeli conflict, and acting as the main obstacle to resolving them sooner rather than later.

Although the Muslim Brotherhood established cells in the 1930s and 1940s in Palestine, the Palestinian nationalist movement took, by and large, a secular direction, and it was mostly after the 1967 war that the Brotherhood found the opportunity to expand its popular influence. By the late 1980s, the Muslim Brothers were given the necessary conditions in the first Palestinian *intifada* (uprising) to elevate the Palestinian radical Islamic group Hamas – the acronym for Harakat al-Muqawamah al-Islamiyah (Movement of Islamic Resistance) – as the major Islamist force among the Palestinians in the occupied West Bank and Gaza Strip. Hamas, which also means 'zeal', emerged in December 1987, shortly after the start of the first *intifada*. Hamas's engagement of Israel in a series of guerrilla operations marked the beginning of Islam's gaining political legitimacy among the Palestinians on a scale never seen before. Its goal was the liberation of all Palestinian land and Islamization of Palestinian politics.

Hamas was initially backed by Israel to counter the secularist Palestine Liberation Organization (PLO) under Yasser Arafat, which had been widely recognized as the embodiment of the Palestinian nationalist movement until the start of the *intifada*, but had been rejected by Israel and shunned by the USA as a 'terrorist' organization. However, it rapidly emerged as a strongly anti-Israeli movement, with a special dislike for the USA as a pro-Zionist power. Within a short space of time, operating very much along the lines of the Muslim Brothers (as explained in Chapter 2) Hamas grew in stature and influence beyond anyone's expectations. By 1993, it could claim a following estimated at 30–40 per cent of Palestinians in the occupied territories, and attracted moral, political and financial backing from various sources in the Muslim world, including Iran and Saudi Arabia. To boost its position, it drew not only on the PLO's failures and the Palestinians' increased suffering under Israeli occupation, but also on the Islamic grievances of Palestinians and Muslims in general. Hamas captured the sentiment of many radical Islamists and ordinary Muslims inside and outside the Palestinian territories when

it proclaimed that '*jihad* [in this case holy war] is the "personal obli-
gation" of every Muslim, for Palestine [is] the "soil of Islamic trust
till the end of days"' and denounced Jews as 'an instrument of evil
that turns the wheels of history'.[29]

Feeling threatened more by Hamas than by the PLO, and backed
by the USA, Israel in the end chose the PLO as its 'partner' in the
Oslo peace process, initiated in September 1993. But Hamas and its
smaller sister organization, the Islamic Jihad Movement, in Palestine
and many other similar organizations in the region remained deeply
suspicious of the process and the USA's rejectionist attitude towards
them. It is important to note that Islamic Jihad, which surfaced as an
operational group in 1987, also had its origin, like Hamas and several other similar militant Islamic groups in the Middle East, in the
Muslim Brotherhood. However, being a Palestinian group, its ideology and practices have been tied to the Palestinian nationalist cause.
It has been linked to Lebanese Hezbullah and Iranian Hezbullahis,
and has operated in tandem with Hamas, although remaining much
smaller both organizationally and operationally.[30] The advent since
October 2000 of the Palestinians' second (or Al-Quds) *intifada*
against continued repressive Israeli occupation has further led to the
emergence of another militant group, the Al-Aqsa Brigade, which
also deploys Islam as an ideology of resistance, and is thought to be
an offshoot of the PLO's main group, Fateh. All three groups have
been active in suicide bombings against Israeli military and civilian
targets, which in turn has attracted massive Israeli retaliation and
reoccupation of most Palestinian towns and cities, where control had
previously been transferred under the Oslo process to the Palestinian
Authority, led by Arafat.

From the perspective of Palestinian and most other radical
Islamists, the US strategic partnership with Israel has been critical in
enabling the Jewish state to defy resolution of the Palestinian problem.
It is their view that the USA's maintenance of a monopoly on the
Middle East peace process has largely been designed to protect
Israel. They have been deeply disenchanted by the USA's double
standard – one approach for Israel and another for Arabs – and emo-
tionally charged by US vetoes of UN Security Council resolutions
critical of Israel and by Washington's reluctance to pressure Israel as
it has pressured Arabs to abide by UN resolutions and international
laws and norms. For example, it is of deep concern for Muslims that
the USA has insisted Iraq must implement UN resolutions or remain

under UN sanctions, but has put no similar pressure on Israel. They have shared the disdain of many of their secular counterparts, including disarmament specialists, for the approach by the USA and its allies to the problem of weapons of mass destruction (WMD) in the region. They argue that while Israel has WMD capabilities, Washington's emphasis is on depriving Arabs and Iranians of WMD. Washington's argument that Israel can be trusted, being a democracy, with a responsible system of command and control, but Arabs and the Iranians are not to be trusted, especially as Saddam Hussein used chemical weapons against his own Kurdish population in 1988, does not wash well with most Arab and Iranian Islamists and nationalists. Their counter-argument is that Israel is only a conditional democracy, determined not only to be an occupying power, but also to use its conventional military might to maintain this occupation. They contend that if the USA really wants the region free of WMD, it must press for a region-wide regime of arms control, including Israel – something the USA has not been prepared to do. They are equally perturbed by Washington's unwavering support for Israel's right of 'self-defence', unmatched by any endorsement of a Palestinian right to self-defence against Israeli occupation.

Fundamentally, they argue that the USA cannot be a strategically of Israel and an impartial peace broker at the same time. This view has never previously gained as much potency as in the current confrontation between the Israelis and Palestinians, over which the United States and Israel have been condemned in almost equal terms in the region and beyond for Israel's use of excessive force against mostly unarmed Palestinians. Their concerns have resonated well among the Muslim masses, especially among the many Arabs who have organic ties with the Palestinians and view the Palestinian humiliation as their own. This, together with the way the USA backed UN sanctions against Iraq have affected the ordinary Iraqi people instead of Saddam Hussein's regime, has generated much anguish among the Arabs and helped radical Islamic groups to serve as the channel for expressing it against not only the USA, but also their own pro-US governments. It is ironic that Arab countries such as Egypt, the United Arab Emirates and Saudi Arabia, where the USA has had the greatest political and economic influence, are also the ones where the USA has become the focus of greatest public discontent. According to various indicators, anti-US sentiment has never been as strong among the ordinary citizens of these countries and other Arab states as it is now. One way through which this sentiment was expressed prior to the events of September 11 was for some wealthy citizens, especially in the Gulf, where an estimated $500 billion is in the hands of private Saudis alone, to give Islamic alms (Zakat) to the Taliban and Al Qaeda, not because they identified with their causes, but because of their anti-US stand. This also explains Washington's post-September 11 decision to monitor closely such transfers, and the activities of many Islamic charity organizations, and the subsequent banning of several of them as related to international terrorism.

Afghanistan

The third issue over which many Islamists and ordinary Muslims have grown wary of the USA (and for that matter of some US allies) has been the Afghan conflict. This has been closely related to the US counter-intervention strategy in addressing the Soviet occupation of Afghanistan in the 1980s and its total neglect of post-communist Afghanistan. The Soviet invasion of Afghanistan in late December 1979 essentially confirmed the hostility many Muslims held towards atheist communism, and perceived Russian/Soviet historical ambitions towards the region south of the USSR, in the direction of the Persian Gulf and Indian Ocean. This was also an event that the USA, and to a lesser extent other Soviet Western adversaries, as well as the People's Republic of China, immediately utilized to limit and, if possible, defeat Soviet power. However, in this instance Washington found it opportune to let realpolitik rather than ideological preferences determine its counter-interventionist strategy.

In contrast to the Iranian case, Washington showed no moral or political qualms in welcoming the deployment of Islam as an ideology of resistance to Soviet occupation. It immediately embraced various Afghan Islamic resistance forces, the Mujahideen, a mixture of radical and moderate groups, divided by personality, sectarian, tribal, ethnic and linguistic differences.[31] It also readopted Pakistan as a frontline ally against Soviet communism, after nearly a decade of frost between the two sides because of Pakistan's withdrawal in 1973 from CENTO, and America's shift of priorities to focus on the Vietnam War. In the process, it also embraced the reassertively Islamic military dictatorship of General Zia ul-Haq to serve as a conduit, through whose military intelligence (ISI) the USA could supply aid to the Mujahideen groups. However, it did so on one condition – that these groups, like the Saudi regime, remain directly or indirectly under US influence.

The USA confined its support to the main groups drawn from the majority Sunni Muslim population of Afghanistan and based in Pakistan, thus avoiding any action which might help the Iranian-Shi'ite Mujahideen groups or Iranian Islamic regime. It aided whatever Sunni group came forward to fight the Soviet occupation and was endorsed by the ISI. It displayed little understanding of the nature of Islam in Afghanistan, which had never been extreme, but was vulnerable to manipulation under the right circumstances. The CIA was given prime responsibility for the conduct of America's proxy war. In close alliance with ISI, the CIA funded arms not only for thousands of Afghans, but also for hundreds of Muslims from Pakistan and the Arab world to join the Afghans in a *jihad* against the Soviets and their surrogates. While Saudi Arabia – a traditional Islamic friend of Pakistan, well disposed towards General Zia ul-Haq's re-Islamization – provided much of the needed capital, the CIA developed contacts with various Islamic groups and an international network of Islamic activists, some more radical and traditionalist than others, including some based in the USA, to support the USA's Afghan counter-intervention.[32]

The USA's virtually unqualified support of Pakistan proved fraught with peril from the start. Regardless of Pakistan's chronically fragile domestic structures, disastrous economic and social conditions, continued military entrenchment in politics, and mounting problems of national identity and direction, Washington paid little attention to how its policies might affect Pakistan and the region in the medium to long run. As things turned out, they proved harmful in many ways. They significantly assisted the military regime of President General Zia ul-Haq to overcome the illegitimacy of its usurpation of power in 1977 and execution in 1979 of former Prime Minister Zulfiqar Ali Bhutto, whom Zia had deposed. They also aided the regime to ensure its longevity, based on a politics of public deception, divide and rule, and re-Islamization of Pakistan, and camouflage its drive to acquire nuclear weapons capability. This, together with Zia's granting of almost unlimited powers to the ISI to handle Pakistan's Afghanistan and Kashmir policies, created a terrible legacy. On the one hand, it entrenched the culture of the military and secret service in Pakistani politics, and on the other, it encouraged the growth of Islamic militancy and sectarian violence. Islamic militants, associated with Jamaati Islami Pakistan, Jamiati Ulama-i Islam and a number of other groups that developed under ISI patronage, found a new political legitimacy to enhance their positions in Pakistani politics, participate in the Afghan *jihad* against the Soviets, and join an international network of activists, involving hundreds of Arabs.

The ISI effectively tapped into this network not only to have a major hand in the Afghan Islamic resistance, but also to drum up the cause of Kashmiri separatists against India, and link up with different Islamic movements and groups in the region and beyond. This development severely impaired the ability of those civilian leaders who came to power after Zia ul-Haq's death in an air crash in August 1988 to put Pakistan on a stable course of democratization, and eventually helped the military to regain power under General Pervez Musharraf in the coup of October 1999. It also generated many state sponsored radical Islamic forces in Pakistan, some of which became inextricably linked to various Afghan Mujahideen and Kashmiri Islamic groups, including Harakatul Ansar, or what later was renamed Harakatul Mujahideen.

In this context, the US government soon became entangled with several forces whose use of Islam for extremist purposes was bound to have serious repercussions for the future of Afghanistan and many other countries, including some US allies in the region.[33] One such group, which emerged as more extremist in both its ideological and policy disposition than many of its counterparts in the Muslim world, was the Hezbi Islami Afghanistan (Islamic Party of Afghanistan), led by Gulbuddin Hekmatyar. A self-styled Islamist, and a highly political opportunist, with unbounded power ambitions, Hekmatyar was the most maverick of his kind. He was a Pashtun, therefore a member of Afghanistan's largest (if highly tribalized) ethnic cluster. Both the Mohammedzai clan of the Durrani tribe that ruled Afghanistan for most of the time from the foundation of modern Afghanistan in 1847 until the communist coup of 1978, and subsequently the bulk of the Taliban, came from this cluster. Hekmatyar not only caused much conflict and bloodshed within the Afghan resistance, and subsequently destroyed half of Kabul at the cost of thousands of lives when he could not seize power following the communist regime's collapse in April 1992, but also practised the worst deeds he could justify in the name of Islam, with special antipathy toward the West. At times, he publicly condemned the USA as an evil power, and refused to meet US political leaders for fear of compromising his orthodoxy. Yet, for most of the 1980s, he was courted by Washington, and received the lion's share of American military assistance to the Mujahideen. Washington was repeatedly warned about him, but to little avail. Because he was the favourite of the ISI, which wanted him to head a pro-Pakistani post-communist government in Kabul, he was also treated as good for Washington, as long as he was under Pakistan's control and served US interests.[34]

In a similar vein, Washington allowed its counter-interventionist activities to favour a variety of Arab volunteers from various countries, ranging from Saudi Arabia to Egypt to Algeria. One of these volunteers was Osama Bin Laden, a well-educated, rich Saudi, with an estimated wealth of $250 million and access to many private sources of donations in the Gulf Arab states. Bin Laden first came to Afghanistan in 1984, and joined a Mujahideen training camp in the Afghan eastern province of Nangarhar, under the watchful eyes of the ISI, which at the time worked intimately with the CIA. He soon emerged not only as an Arab *jihadi* hero, but also, by the turn of the 1990s, as a major Islamist opponent of the USA. He came to resent deeply what he viewed as the USA's maintenance of the Saudi regime, subjugation of Islam's holiest land and domination of the region and its oil resources. He also soon came to denounce US support for Israel, its occupation of Palestinian land, especially East Jerusalem, and its suppression of the Palestinian people. He had, as early as 1988, 'reportedly described it as the duty of every Muslim "to prepare himself to defend Mecca and Medina from the 'Jews' " '.[35]

Bin Laden became more vocal in his criticism of the Saudi regime and the USA in the wake of their military response to the August 1990 Iraqi invasion of Kuwait – a response that was launched from Saudi Arabia.[36] Like most Islamists, Bin Laden had little time for Saddam Hussein as a secular and opportunist leader and could not condone his invasion of Kuwait, but he opposed the deployment of US troops on Islam's holy Saudi Arabian soil to fight a fellow Arab state. The Saudi regime stripped him of his citizenship; after a short stay in Sudan, he returned in 1996 through Pakistan to a changed Afghanistan, this time not to resist the long-departed Soviets, but to achieve wider purposes.[37]

In addition to Bin Laden, other elements spawned into Islamic radicalism in the context of US counter-interventionist policies were Arab fighters who participated in the Afghan resistance, and upon returning to their native countries, took up arms against their secularist governments. Two prime examples have been the Islamic militants in Algeria and Egypt, many of whom are reportedly veterans of the Afghan Islamic resistance.

Of course, this does not mean that their struggles have no real local causes. On the contrary, in Algeria, where their operations (some in the most gruesome form imaginable) resulted in more than 100,000 deaths in the 1990s, the militants' grievances are rooted in the military's cancellation of the February 1992 elections, which the Islamic Salvation Front (FIS) was poised to win. Yet, it is also undeniably true that many militant FIS supporters had fought in Afghanistan under the guidance and supervision of the ISI and CIA, and had become involved in the wider network of Islamic militants whose growth was encouraged by US policies. Washington's conspicuous silence over the military's cancellation of the Algerian elections only rubbed salt in the wound as far as these militants were concerned. The case of the Egyptian Islamic militants, some of whom, such as the members of Islamic Jihad, joined Bin Laden, is similar. Although the Egyptian authorities have now succeeded in containing their bloody operations, which included killing hundreds of foreign tourists during the 1990s, there remains the possibility that they could be nourished again by their international linkages at an appropriate time.

All this certainly helped the USA to achieve its prime goal of defeating the Soviets in Afghanistan, thus paying them back for their support of the victors in Vietnam. The Soviets withdrew ignominiously from Afghanistan in 1989, as the USA had from Vietnam in 1975. Both the USSR and USA retained, under the Afghan Geneva Accords of 1988 (signed between Pakistan and the Soviet installed government of Najibullah in Kabul and guaranteed by the two superpowers), the right to continue assisting their Afghan clients. However, the Soviet Union's disintegration in late 1991, to which the USSR's Afghan fiasco in part contributed,[38] left Najibullah's government high and dry; by April 1992 it had collapsed. Yet the ISI's main protégé, Hekmatyar, was neither popular nor strong enough to take over Kabul and establish his own Islamic government. To ISI's total disappointment, the victory went to Hekmatyar's Tajik rival, the highly independent minded, moderate Islamist and ardent nation-alist Commander Ahmed Shah Massoud from the Panjshir Valley north of Kabul. Massoud was a key figure in the first Mujahideen government, which, as had earlier been agreed among Pakistan based Mujahideen leaders, was initially headed for two months by a Pashtun resistance leader, Sebghtullah Mujadidi, and then from June 1992 by Burhanuddin Rabbani, the political head of the resistance group Jamiati Islami Afghanistan (the Islamic Society of Afghanistan) to which Massoud belonged. Hekmatyar was offered the prime minis-tership for the sake of unity, but refused to take it up because he wanted to become the unchallenged Amir or ruler of Afghanistan. Instead, he started rocketing Kabul from mid-1992, killing some 25,000 people, destroying nearly half the city over a year and a half, and effectively preventing the Rabbani–Massoud government from consolidating power. Hekmatyar's failure to wrest power, despite all ISI support and alliances with the Uzbek warlord Rashid Dostum and the Iranian-backed Shi'ite Hezbi Wahdat from late 1993, made him a liability for Pakistan.

Once the Soviets withdrew and their surrogate government in Kabul collapsed, Washington saw its ultimate goal as achieved. With no concern for the Afghan people's future, it simply turned its back on Afghanistan, and left the ISI and its array of Islamic activists to do whatever they liked. Given this and Hekmatyar's proven useless-ness, the ISI deemed it desirable to raise a fresh extremist Islamic Sunni Pashtun militia to take over power in Afghanistan. That militia was the Taliban, which burst onto the Afghan scene in late 1994. The ISI's objectives were clear: to secure for Pakistan a receptive government in Kabul, a favourable final conclusion to the historical Afghan–Pakistan border dispute, some strategic depth in Afghanistan against India, and strong leverage for wider regional influence, especially in the wake of the Soviet Union's disintegration and the opening up of a new, potentially resource and market rich Muslim Central Asia.

The main driving force behind the Taliban was originally Pakistani General Nasreellah Babar, Minister of Interior in the first government of Prime Minister Benazir Bhutto, who won the first general election after Zia ul-Haq's death. It is reported that it was Babar who con-ceived the Taliban (Islamic Students) idea and made it operational by selecting a former Mujahideen fighter from among the Pashtuns of southern Afghanistan, Mullah Mohammed Omar, to lead a force of

Afghan and Pakistani Pashtuns. This force was ostensibly formed to protect a Pakistani commercial convoy heading for Central Asia against Mujahideen warlords in various parts of the country, who were often independent of the Rabbani government in Kabul, and often in conflict with one another. The success of this group encouraged Babar and his ISI cohorts to enlarge it into a formidable force to take over Afghanistan. Young Afghan Pashtun refugees and Pakistani students studying in various Pakistani religious schools (*madrasas*) financed by Saudi Arabia and influenced by Wahabi Islam (which since the nineteenth century had intersected with the puritanic Deobandi school of Islam in northern India) provided the Taliban's foot soldiers. The task of supervising and directing the Taliban was entrusted to the ISI. The Taliban essentially embodied a medievalist and highly discriminatory form of neofundamentalist Islam, with the harshest treatment reserved for women and Shi'ites.[39] They immediately imposed their rule in the areas they conquered, instituting a theocracy that Afghans had never before experienced.[40]

While the Taliban leaders, who were very narrowly educated, may have been genuinely devoted to this kind of Islam and Islamic rule, for the ISI the Taliban phenomenon was a geopolitical instrument for wider ends. However, for the Taliban to succeed, they needed far more resources than Pakistan could provide covertly. That is where US acquiescence in ISI actions, and financial support from Saudi Arabia, the United Arab Emirates and Bin Laden's alliance mattered critically.

Washington knew from the start about Pakistan's promotion of the Taliban, as Benazir Bhutto, who approved of ISI's initiative at the time, has intimated on several occasions. It apparently supported the Taliban for two main reasons. One was the argument that the Taliban was primarily an anti-Shi'ite, and therefore anti-Iranian, militia. This also appealed to two of the USA's Arab allies, given Saudi Arabia's regional rivalry with Iran and the United Arab Emirates' dispute with Iran over three islands in the Gulf. In fact, Riyadh and Abu Dhabi initially bankrolled the Taliban and Pakistan's efforts in support of it, and subsequently joined Pakistan in recognizing the Taliban as Afghanistan's legitimate government. Another was the impression that the Taliban would bring stability to Afghanistan, opening a direct route from Pakistan to Central Asia, where Washington was concerned to block a perceived upsurge in Iranian influence, and through which US companies could export oil and gas from Central Asia, especially gas from Turkmenistan, to South Asia and beyond.

These factors were instrumental in enabling the Taliban to take over Kabul, with full Pakistani support, by September 1996, dislodging the Rabbani–Massoud government to the north.[41]

At about that time Bin Laden arrived back in Afghanistan. What he brought was his wealth, his credentials as an Arab Islamist – always held in high esteem by non-Arab Islamists, given the status of the Arabs as the original recipients of Islam – and Arab connections, which boosted the fortunes of both the Taliban and their Pakistani patrons. Bin Laden immediately became the esteemed 'guest' of the Taliban, although he and Taliban leader Mullah Mohammed Omar had no previous connections. With ISI patronage of him as well as of the Taliban, Bin Laden rapidly expanded his network of followers and activists, who could get in and out of Afghanistan only through Pakistan, given the hostility to the Taliban of Afghanistan's other neighbours. In 1997, his efforts in helping the Taliban and broadening Al Qaeda's network received a major boost when the Egyptian Islamic Jihad, led by Ayman Al-Zawahiri, merged with Al Qaeda. By now a clear axis had been forged between the Taliban, Al Qaeda and ISI.

Having defeated or bought off most former Mujahideen commanders, the only resistance this axis faced was that mounted by Massoud and his supporters, who controlled the Shomali plains north of Kabul, the Panjshir Valley, and parts of north-eastern Afghanistan. They were mostly cut off from the outside world, and the best Massoud could do was maintain the resistance on a scale consonant with his limited resources and exhausted fighters, do whatever necessary to maintain and expand an anti-Taliban alliance of various desperate factions, his own the largest and dominant one, and keep appealing to the international community to stop Pakistan's creeping takeover and the Taliban–Al Qaeda transformation of Afghanistan into a threat to regional and international stability.

Massoud repeatedly called on the USA and its allies to take seriously the gravity of the Afghan situation and back his resistance to the ominous alliance being forged between a non-Arab extremist militia, an Arab militant network and a state intelligence service. However, his warnings fell on deaf ears in Washington, which persisted with a policy of no assistance to any Afghan faction.

Washington seemed to view the Taliban, at least until the end of 1997, as beneficial to US interests. Its anti-Iranian character and purported ability to secure a direct corridor through Afghanistan to former Soviet Central Asian Muslim republics appeared appealing.

Just as Washington had failed to see the immediate consequences of its disengagement from Afghanistan, it paid no attention to the possible medium to long term consequences. Tacitly, if not actively, it encouraged various US companies to participate in projects designed to access Central Asia's energy resources through Afghanistan, and in the process enrich the Taliban to strengthen and perpetuate its theocracy. A consortium that attracted widespread attention because of its favourable disposition towards the Taliban was led by UNOCAL of the USA and Delta Oil of Saudi Arabia, which proposed to construct a $2.5 billion pipeline across Afghanistan to export gas from Turkmenistan to South Asia. Washington's main concern was to deny Iran a role as an alternative route. It paid no more than lip service to the international outcry over the Taliban's brutal and regressive reign of terror, involving massive human rights violations. Similarly, it remained mute in the face of growing reports that the Taliban and its cohorts were transforming Afghanistan into a major source of opium, heroin production and drug trafficking, the proceeds of which were used to help finance their relentless war against the opposition.[42]

The USA generally sidelined reports about ISI-driven Taliban and Al Qaeda training of Arab and Kashmiri militants to fight 'US hegemony' in the Muslim world and India's control of Jammu and Kashmir. It refused to castigate publicly Taliban–Bin Laden extremism or Pakistan's support for it, or to recognize that the armed opposition led by Massoud was essential to block a complete Pakistani–Taliban–Al Qaeda takeover of Afghanistan. Although Al Qaeda had commenced large-scale operations, targeting the Egyptian Embassy in Islamabad in early 1997 at the cost of many lives, Washington remained content to voice only occasional verbal disapproval of some Taliban policies. Its strongest disapproval came at the end of 1997 when finally, under pressure from US lobbyists in support of Afghan women, Secretary of State Albright, said: 'we are opposed to the Taliban ... [b]ecause of their approach to human rights, their treatment of women and children and their general lack of respect for human dignity'. She also said that the USA believed the Taliban was not 'in a position' to occupy all of Afghanistan. 'There are other parties', she went on, 'who need to be recognized and there needs to be a government that is composed of them'.[43] As the situation developed, this was a foretaste of wider American criticisms in the months to come.

Even so, had it not been for Bin Laden's masterminding of the bombing of US Embassies in Kenya and Tanzania, with hundreds of casualties, in August 1998, Washington would likely have remained disengaged from developments in Afghanistan. The embassy bombings brought the 'chickens home to roost' for both the USA and Saudi Arabia, and jolted Washington out of its slumber. It now viewed the developments in Afghanistan as damaging and found it imperative to act. In the first instance, the Clinton Administration promptly launched two cruise missile attacks – one on what the USA described as a Bin Laden-linked chemical weapons factory in Sudan, and another on Bin Laden's training camps in eastern Afghanistan. The first target turned out to be a pharmaceuticals producing plant, with no proven linkage to Bin Laden; the second missed Bin Laden and his top lieutenants, although several of the 24 killed were Kashmiri militant trainees, thus clearly establishing the bonds between Bin Laden, the Taliban and Kashmiri militants, and that the ISI had established close links between various client forces for a wider, multi-faceted regional network of armed activists.

The USA's missile attack did nothing to deter the Taliban and their Arab and Pakistani supporters from continuing their push to conquer all of Afghanistan. Before the end of 1998, the Taliban had not only taken over most of the country, pressuring Massoud from all directions, but also consolidated their terrorist infrastructure beyond anyone's expectations. This infrastructure was critical for Bin Laden to strengthen his Al Qaeda network of Arab and non-Arab activists with global reach, ready to strike at a wide range of US targets. Bin Laden's relations with the Taliban proved so organic that the latter owed him more for their success than he owed them for his protection.

The ISI could only rejoice over the successes of the Bin Laden–Taliban alliance, especially in relation to its goal of achieving 'strategic depth' in Afghanistan against India. It accelerated its efforts to recruit Pakistani and Arab Islamic radicals, Central Asian Islamic opposition elements, such as members of the Uzbekistan Islamic Movement, and Chechen Islamic fighters, to boost the operational capacity of Bin Laden and the Taliban leadership beyond Afghanistan's borders. While the Taliban castigated the secular rulers of the Central Asian republics, declared full support for Chechen independence from Russia, and invited the Chechens to open a diplomatic mission in Kabul, new recruits were trained, armed and commissioned to operate both inside and outside Afghanistan. Their number soon grew into thousands, with 3000 to 5000 Arabs forming Bin Laden's personal army alone.

To capture Bin Laden and break up the Al Qaeda network, Washington's approach, by late 1999, focused on three main objectives: to indict and put a bounty on Bin Laden and demand his extradition by the Taliban; to apply diplomatic pressure to Pakistan to lean on the Taliban to meet the USA's demand; and to pay more attention to Russia's complaint about the Taliban's Islamic threat to the former Soviet Central Asian republics, and to India's outcry about what it called the Pakistan–Taliban–Bin Laden sponsorship of crossborder terrorism in Jammu and Kashmir. However, the approach did not include any assistance to Massoud's forces, even though Washington knew that Pakistani involvement, Bin Laden's money, and Arab and Pakistani recruits in their thousands were rapidly changing the balance of forces on the ground against Massoud's newly formed United Islamic Front for the Liberation of Afghanistan, represented by the ousted Rabbani Islamic Government. The USA still refused to name Pakistan as a state sponsoring terrorism, or to maximize pressure on Pakistani governments to rein in the ISI and deprive Bin Laden, his associates and their Taliban protectors of access to Pakistan's territory, the only outlet through which they could organize overseas operations.

The Clinton Administration seemed to have been gripped by the fear that too much pressure on Pakistan, by now both nuclear armed and virtually bankrupt, could lead it to implode, with the possibility of its nuclear weapons falling into wrong hands. It failed to foresee the more grievous results that its inaction could produce.

However, by October 1999 the USA appeared to be having some success with the elected Pakistani government of Prime Minister Nawaz Sharif, whom Washington had successfully pressured earlier in the year to withdraw the ISI-backed, Taliban-aided Kashmir militants from the Indian side of the line of control and thus halt the Kargil military clash – a confrontation which was in danger of developing into a full-scale war between India and Pakistan. Sharif finally publicly accused the Taliban of destabilizing Pakistan, and contemplated changing Pakistan's Afghanistan policy. But within days he was toppled by the Army Joint Chief of Staff, General Pervez Musharraf, who was widely regarded as the architect of the Kargil conflict with India.

General Musharraf initially promised President Clinton, in March 2000, to pressure the Taliban to change direction and hand over Bin Laden, but he soon reneged on the promise. Given the interchangeable relationship between the military and the ISI, and his regime's dependence on these two forces and pro-Taliban Islamic groups, he could not deliver on his promise. By May he was publicly defending Pakistan's support of the Taliban on grounds of 'national security interests'. He urged Washington to enter direct negotiations with the Taliban, and the world community to follow the example of Pakistan, Saudi Arabia and the United Arab Emirates in recognizing it as Afghanistan's legitimate government, even though Riyadh had frozen its relations from late 1998.

Frustrated with Pakistan, and alarmed by the discovery of more anti-American terrorist plots by elements allegedly related to Bin Laden, Washington resolved to up the ante on the Taliban, by responding more warmly to overtures by Moscow and New Delhi for closer policy coordination against international terrorism, a development which gained wider potency following the hijacking in late 1999 of an Indian passenger airliner by Kashmiri militants in apparent collusion with the ISI and the Taliban, and the suspected bombing by Al Qaeda of the USS *Cole* off the coast of Aden, which killed a number of the crew and disabled the ship. In November 1999, Washington, jointly with Moscow, sponsored UN Security Council Resolution 1267, imposing limited economic sanctions on the Taliban, followed a year later by Resolution 1333 which tightened the sanctions and added an arms embargo; this was complemented by Resolution 1363 in July 2001, endorsing the stationing of monitors in neighbouring countries, especially Pakistan.

However, these measures proved ineffective, given the Taliban's defiance and Pakistan's blatant violations. They did little to moderate the Taliban's behaviour or make Pakistan change direction. If anything, the more measures the UN passed, the more the Taliban and their ISI minders riposted with provocative counter-measures to impress upon the international community that the Taliban were in charge of Afghanistan and they should deal with it directly. These ripostes included the destruction of all pre-Islamic statues and artefacts, most importantly the two gigantic Bamiyan Buddhas; closing UN-run bakeries which provided bread for numerous destitute Kabul families; the requirement that the tiny Hindu minority wear distinctive yellow badges; and finally the arrest of eight Western aid workers and 16 of their Afghan support staff on charges of promoting Christianity. These outraged the international community, yet at the same time forced it to interact with the Taliban. Musharraf's government played, at best, a dubious role in all this. While publicly calling on the Taliban to moderate the counter-measures, it kept criticizing the UN steps, and urged the international community to engage rather than isolate the Taliban, rejected criticism of Pakistan's role in Afghanistan, and maintained its façade of military non-involvement.

The problem with the US strategy was that it mostly focused on judicial means, diplomatic pressure and a couple of attempted covert military operations for one, and only one, purpose: to capture Bin Laden and his top aides. It failed to see that Bin Laden and his Al Qaeda network were closely intertwined with the Taliban and the ISI, that Bin Laden virtually owned the Taliban by providing it with millions of dollars and thousands of Arab fighters, and that there was little chance of taking out Bin Laden and his Al Qaeda lieutenants without simultaneously taking on the Taliban and the ISI. It also paid only transitory attention to the wider brutalities of these three forces against the Afghan people. Massoud and his United Front partners were frustrated and disappointed by the narrow, and in many ways, futile US approach.

To Massoud, the only way forward was for the USA and the international community to deal with the source of the problem: Pakistan's ISI and military leadership. Disenchanted with what he saw as US indifference towards the Afghan tragedy, Massoud found it imperative to continue to broaden the resistance in whatever way possible, as the only means of pressuring the Taliban and Pakistan to opt for a negotiated settlement of the Afghan conflict, provide for formation of a broad-based multi-ethnic government, remove terrorist networks from Afghanistan, and curtail Pakistan's 'creeping invasion'. In the first half of 2000, he made relentless efforts to expand the opposition by incorporating more former Mujahideen leaders into it, so as to open more fronts, and thus prevent the Taliban–Arab–Pakistani forces concentrating against his fighters alone. He welcomed back into the resistance two former provincial governors, Ismail Khan of Herat, who had escaped from a Taliban prison a year earlier, and Haji Abdul Qadir of Nangarhar, and the Uzbek warlord, General Rashid Dostum, despite Dostum's past human rights abuses. While his United Front (or the so-called Northern Alliance) was largely made up of non-Pashtuns, it contained at least two Pashtun Mujahideen leaders, Abdul Rasul Sayaf and Haji Abdul Qadir, as well as a number of Pashtun commanders.

This, together with some financial assistance and arms that Massoud received from India, Iran and Russia, helped him to frustrate his opponents. He had been the target of many Taliban–Pakistani assassination attempts, but finally, just when he was ready to go on the offensive in the final weeks of the northern autumn of 2001, his enemies succeeded in eliminating him through an act of terrorism. He was killed by two Arabs, who posed as a journalist and cameraman, but were actually Al Qaeda operatives. As the Taliban chief of intelligence subsequently stated, the operatives had direct orders from Bin Laden to eliminate Massoud ahead of the network's September 11 attacks, so that the USA would have no allies inside Afghanistan for retaliatory purposes. Massoud left a number of excellent commanders and a solid military structure, and his death did not seriously affect the morale and fighting capability of his forces, which proved very effective when the USA and its allies launched their anti-terrorist war against the Taliban and Al Qaeda. Not only did they provide the USA with the necessary bridgehead and spearheaded most of the ground fighting, but their now younger leadership, composed of Massoud's successor, Mohammed Fahim, and Massoud's foreign and internal affairs chiefs, Dr Abdullah Abdullah and Yonous Qanooni respectively, in November 2001 successfully negotiated with three other groups the Bonn agreement for an Interim Administration to replace the Taliban government.

The Clinton Administration undoubtedly made some visible efforts during its second term to correct some of the USA's past mistakes in its dealings with the Muslim world, and introduced some perceptive changes in US policy behaviour. While still maintaining that adversarial forces of political Islam threatened Western interests, it endeavoured to be less belligerent towards them than its predecessors. It came to accept that although these forces share a common faith, they are nonetheless divided along sectarian, cultural, social and political lines, reflecting in their attitudes and operations more their individual local causes and circumstantial imperatives than a common Islamic cause. For example, whereas Hamas and Islamic Jihad (both Sunni) have thrived very much on the Palestinian cause against Israel, Hezbullah (Shi'ite) has been very Lebanese in its opposition to Israel. Yet none of them has had any clear links with the

Algerian Islamic Salvation Front, the Taliban, or the Kashmiri Harakat al-Mujahideen. Even Hezbullah's links with the Iranian Islamic regime are now clearly more with the hardline faction than with the moderates within that regime.

Furthermore, the Clinton Administration came to recognize the futility of 'dual containment' and the growing popularity of the Iranian Islamic reformists, led by President Mohammed Khatami. It voiced support for his reforms and his call for better relations between the people of Iran and the USA, based on dialogue rather than 'clash of civilizations'. In addition, the Clinton Administration worked harder than its predecessors to remove or diminish some of the anomalies in US foreign policy towards the Israelis and Arabs, making serious efforts to achieve a solution of the Israeli–Palestinian conflict.

However, it could not produce the desired results, for two main reasons. One was that President Clinton began his efforts too late in his second term and when his position was much undermined by personal scandals, which in turn provided little incentive to the parties he wished to engage to respond positively to his approaches. This was the case with the Iranian as well as the Israeli and Palestinian leaderships, although in the case of Iran the fact that hardliners from both sides had become too entrenched did not help. Another reason, was related specifically to the Israeli–Palestinian dispute: as long as the USA maintained its strategic alliance with Israel and East Jerusalem remained under sole Israeli control, Clinton could not expect a major breakthrough.

Clinton's Republican successor, George W. Bush, commenced his presidency in an aura of international defiance and global supremacy. Instead of building on some of Clinton's initiatives to address the root causes of anti-Americanism in the Arab and Muslim world, his administration focused mainly on those issues which could underscore the US position as the world's leading power. He had made it clear well before the September 11 events that he had little time for Iranian Islamic radicalism and for the Palestinian *intifada*, or for the Palestinian leader, Yasser Arafat, whom Sharon had already started accusing of being behind the *intifada* – an issue which is discussed in the final chapter.

Although these three developments emerged from different bases and produced different outcomes, they highlight the danger of inadequate sensitivity to the Muslim world's complexities by the USA and other Western states which have been content to follow the US lead. It is clear that Iranian Islamic radicalism, Afghan Islamic resistance, and Palestinian Islamic assertiveness interacted to induce an unprecedented degree of radicalization among Muslims, who remain divided politically but have projected a semblance of religious unity. Ultimately, Washington's handling of them goes some distance towards explaining why this radicalization has from time to time spawned an anti-US, and to some extent general anti-Western, upsurge in the Muslim world. The US's approach to these developments from the start was contradictory, naïve and self-centred, devoid of any deep consideration of long term consequences. It showed little or no concern about the manner in which US policy actions could negatively affect the lives of ordinary Muslims, or their perceptions of, and relations with, the West. Nor did it pay much attention to the way in which the USA's policy behaviour could play into the hands of elements on both sides who for political and ideological reasons want relations to remain disrupted and confrontational.

Against this backdrop, the atrocious September 11 attacks materialized, and Bin Laden and his Al Qaeda network were able to draw not only considerable vocal sympathy from Islamic radicals but also an amount of tacit understanding from many ordinary Muslims. This is not to suggest that a majority of Muslims are set to side with Bin Laden and his fanatic activists, and least of all with the Taliban, whose rule was violently opposed even in Afghanistan. But what it does convey is that there are numerous anti-US grievances in the Muslim world that Bin Laden and his supporters were able to tap to boost recruitment and support. It also indicates that US use of force would be insufficient on its own to achieve its anti-terror objectives. It needs to be accompanied by an elaborate political strategy to deal with some of the grievances which have given rise to terrorism, and which cannot be resolved by military might alone. Yet the responsibility must not be entirely placed on the USA. Many of the grievances have indigenous roots, and can be largely related to the lack of democracy in the Muslim world in general, and its Arab components in particular.

5

Democracy and Authoritarianism

As an ideal of government, democracy has been as much a catchcry in the domain of Islam since the Second World War, and more intensely since the end of the Cold War, as in most other parts of the world. Whatever their degrees of commitment to it, most Muslim state leaders have adopted the *vocabulary* of democracy as a useful means of claiming political legitimation and branding their regimes as popular, representing the will of the majority of their respective publics. Many have pointed to the existence of *some* forms of 'popular representation' and 'electoral legitimacy' to substantiate their claim to popular sovereignty and ultimately a democratic system of governance. Yet, in all Muslim countries – notwithstanding the examples of Bangladesh and, of late, Indonesia and Iran, as well as Turkey's 'secular Islam' – what has transpired is a form of absolutism, overt authoritarianism, or veiled authoritarianism. This has been instrumental in perpetuating a serious rift between the ruling elites and ordinary citizens, with the latter locked in a continued syndrome of alienation in relation to public authorities. It has also provided the critical nexus between the domestic and international critics of regimes in the Muslim world. The problem has produced serious consequences in terms of relations between state and society and for human development, and stems from a set of complex, interrelated factors.

The Concept of Democracy

Needless to say, democracy is an overloaded concept. Historically, it has meant different things to different people. It has been applied to many different formations, and in interaction with different socio-cultural traditions and practices has produced diverse forms of government – some more representative, participatory and stable than others. Even in Western democracies, there is no consensus as to precisely what the concept means and how best to express it as an ideal. There is not even widespread agreement among theorists and practitioners as to whether democracy is a form of government, a method of *choosing* a government, or a term applied to a whole society, as intimated in Alexis de Tocqueville's study of *Democracy in America*, which is essentially about American society.[1] Whatever the diversity of views, there is nonetheless a core or minimalist definition that lies beneath all the interpretations and uses of the term. As Anthony Arblaster writes, this core definition

> is necessarily general and vague enough to make such variations possible, but it is not so vague as to permit just any meaning what-soever to be placed on the word. At the root of all definitions of democracy, however refined and complex, lies the idea of popular power, of a situation in which power, and perhaps authority too, rests with the people. That power or authority is usually thought of as being political, and often therefore takes the form of an idea of popular sovereignty – the people as the ultimate political power. But it need not be exclusively political.[2]

By the same token, democracy is a process of public participation whereby power and authority can be transferred in an orderly and peaceful fashion from one popularly mandated leader or party to the next, without the upheaval and bloodshed that often characterize such a transfer in non-democratic systems. Obviously, the institution-al mechanisms and processes for achieving this minimalist position can vary from country to country: they can be either electoral or non-electoral, although election through universal suffrage is often regarded as the best means.

Problems of Democratization

Regimes in the Muslim world, more specifically in the Middle East, have constantly come under domestic and external pressure, especially from the West, to conform at least to this minimalist position as a foundation for the development of a pluralist, tolerant and stable society. The result has been a kaleidoscope of political forms. If one adopts the principles of popular power and popular sovereignty as minimal for instituting democracy, the Iranian regime under both the Shah and his clerical successors, and several other Muslim states, most noticeably Egypt, Jordan, Yemen, Kuwait, Bahrain, Indonesia and Malaysia, can argue that they have made some progress in this respect. They can claim some forms of progress in establishing electoral and representative processes of popular legitimation, whereby citizens are given the opportunity to participate, either directly as in the case of Iran since the revolution of 1978–79, Yemen since its reunification in 1990, Malaysia since its independence, or directly and indirectly as in the case of Egypt, especially since 1981, and Indonesia after the fall of Suharto's regime in 1998. While Pakistan has had a very patchy record of 'democratic' rule, Bangladesh can boast the best record of all, and the Jordanians can also claim to have established a more representative legislative body, with a stronger role in making the government accountable, than may be the case with many other countries in the region, although the Jordanian monarch remains in possession of very strong powers.

Kuwait has boasted a kind of Athenian democracy[3] with an electoral system in which some 80,000 Kuwaiti males, who constitute about 13 per cent of the total population, have been allowed to elect a pluralist national assembly. Further, the King of Bahrain, Sheikh Hamad bin Isa Al Khalifa, who succeeded his father in mid-2001 and changed his title from Emir to King in early 2002, has also taken some steps towards creating a multi-party parliamentary system – something which is also promised by the Emir of Qatar. Meanwhile, such closed regimes as those in Syria, Libya, Tunisia and the Central Asian Muslim states also have resorted to establishing the vestiges of such processes, so as to be able to mount a claim to popular power and authority. Despite the patriarchal nature of societies and the religious and traditional limitations placed on women in these countries, women in all of them, with the exception of Kuwait, have been allowed to participate in the electoral processes. The only Muslim countries where political systems have remained very traditional, with no processes in place to regulate the relations between power holders and the subjects, are Saudi Arabia, the United Arab Emirates and, to some extent, the Sultanate of Oman, and Brunei.

However, a close scrutiny reveals that in most cases their claims to democratic credentials have been purely rhetorical and void of substance in meeting even minimal criteria of democratic credibility. When prompted to promote democratic reforms, a majority of leaderships have done so on a highly selective and exclusive basis, and within procedural frameworks which have not substantially affected their personal or family or elite powers. They have conveniently designed the reforms in such a way as to produce nothing more than systems that may be termed 'democratic in form but authoritarian in content', ensuring that the basic liberal principles of separation of powers, political pluralism, and individual rights and freedoms are not secured against the open-ended, arbitrary needs of rulers. Thus, whether operating within a traditional or traditional-modernist or revolutionary-modernist mould, they have shown a marked reluctance to venture in the direction of creating liberal polities.

The few regimes that have sought to approach even the minimalist position, out of either genuine reformist conviction or domestic and outside pressure, have fallen well short of creating a widely inclusive and competitive system. They have sought to exclude from the process the groups which they have perceived as popularly threatening. In consequence, their reforms have frequently resulted in political polarization and violent conflict – a development which has served as a strong deterrent to others. One can draw on a number of countries' experiences to illustrate this point, but none can be more illustrative than those of Iran, Egypt and Algeria.

The Iranian Experience

As suggested in Chapter 4, in Iran, the whole revolutionary transition from the Shah's pro-Western autocracy to Khomeini's anti-Western (or more specifically, anti-American) 'theo-democracy' provides a clear example of the danger and violence that a process of even limited pro-Western democratization can involve in the Middle East. There is no doubt that a variety of factors, as explained previously, contributed to the creation of a revolutionary situation which eventually caused the Shah's fall. However, with the benefit of hindsight, it is clear that what fatally opened the way for his downfall was his mishandling of the process of limited liberalization as a precondition for democratization of the polity that he sought to implement, especially from 1976.[4]

From the time of his CIA engineered reinstallation on the throne in 1953, the Shah felt it necessary, with Washington's urging, to engage in the kind of policy changes that could popularize his rule. In fact, his entire 'White Revolution' in the 1960s was designed to achieve this purpose. However, he was only prepared to implement political reforms that would not undermine his autocratic powers, while allowing him to assert a commitment to creating a democratic system of government. He focused his reform efforts mainly on those politically-minded or active Iranians who were easy to co-opt and lacked the potential to pose a serious challenge to his powers. This meant that he not only excluded the radical religious and secularist groups from his reforms, but actually directed the reforms against them.

The Shah appeared to believe in the force of intertwined autocratic secularization and modernization as the best way to popularize his rule. In the process, he lost sight of the fact that after four centuries of power struggle between the Shi'ite establishment and political authority in Iran, if his reforms did not have the support of the religious establishment, they were bound to run into difficulty, because the religious establishment was the only force capable of motivating the Iranian public strongly against his reforms. Despite being warned about the danger inherent in his approach, he persisted into the 1970s with a policy of suppressing and marginalizing the religious establishment rather than enticing it to become a genuine participant in his reform endeavours.

Under pressure from the emphasis that President Carter placed on human rights, the Shah inaugurated a phase of what might be called limited liberalization. Although it is not clear what his ultimate goal was, it is evident that he had intended to institute a wider degree of public participation in the policy formulation and policy implementation processes, with a measure of freedom for the people to criticize the government, highlight human rights abuses, and demand greater social justice and equity. While still opposed to dealing with his main opponents in any other than an autocratic manner, he wanted to open avenues of participation for those new social and economic groups that his process of speedy oil based pro-capitalist modernization had generated.

However, in a country where political suppression had been the central instrument of governance for a long time, and the public had not been educated in political pluralism, even this limited amount of reform was sufficient to enable a variety of groups, both old and new, to air their grievances with great ferocity. Yet, while quickly succeeding in instigating a nationwide anti-Shah protest movement by mid-1978, these groups could not develop a shared platform beyond a general desire to overthrow the Shah's regime and hope to replace it with something better. Consequently, following the fall of the Shah in January 1979, the revolutionaries as noted earlier headed in different ideological directions, opening the way for a long, violent power struggle between a cluster of Islamists, whose Shi'ite Islamic message and promises were easily discernible to an overwhelming majority of the Iranian people, and a variety of semi-secularist and secularist groups, whose ideological pronouncements in support of creating a pluralist and liberal system proved bewildering to a large proportion of the Iranian public.

Ayatollah Khomeini and his radical Islamic followers achieved political ascendancy with wide public support, but at the cost of brutally suppressing other groups and demonizing the West with a view to establishing their brand of Shi'ite Islamic government and transforming Iran into an Islamic republic.[5] The regime created an electoral process, but did not establish an inclusive political order. It remained as exclusive and intolerant of opposition as that of the Shah, if not more so, and crushed virtually all forms of organized opposition, giving it no immunity against spontaneous popular uprisings of the kind which initially opened the way for the destruction of the Shah's rule. This, together with the Islamic regime's inability to fulfill its promises of good government and a better life for a majority of Iranians, gave rise to the risk that any future structural political change might be as violent as the one which brought it to power. It was at this juncture that something had to give way. The Islamic hardline or *jihadi* followers of Khomeini, who had long wielded all effective state power, found it imperative to let their *ijtihadi* factional opponents have wider visibility in the system. Hence the election of President Khatami in 1997 and his push for Islamic civil society and democratic reforms. Even so, the *jihadis* have done everything possible to keep a tight lid on the reforms, and make sure that they do not lead to opening up the system in a way that could undermine their own power position and allow secularist reformists to make an inroad into the system. Despite Khatami's reforms, the Iranian leadership as a whole is still confronted with a dilemma similar to that which faced the Shah in the last years of his rule: to keep the political system exclusive is as dangerous as to make it inclusive.[6]

The Iranian experience in the wake of the violent revolutionary overthrow of the Shah had a lasting political and psychological impact on other leaderships in the region. It taught them to be wary of any degree of democratization which could move them on the same path as that of the Shah. It reinforced the position of those autocratic leaders who had been looking for reasons to uphold their belief in authoritarianism as the most suitable form of governance for their respective countries. It is not surprising to see, for example, the members of the Gulf Cooperation Council, especially Saudi Arabia, as well as many other Muslim states in the Middle East and beyond, showing marked reluctance to take their chances with political reform.

The Egyptian and Algerian Attempts

The Egyptian and Algerian experiences tell somewhat similar stories. In Egypt, during the more than two decades of President Husni Mubarak's rule, a number of steps have been instituted to improve the conditions for wider public participation and popular legitimation, accompanied by a guarantee of some basic individual rights and freedoms. However, Mubarak has ultimately nurtured a presidential system which has concentrated too much power in the executive branch, and more specifically in the hands of an indirectly elected president whose exercise of power has been conditioned more on the traditional support that he has received from the armed and security forces, and business and professional elites, than on direct public consent. The system lacks the necessary operational checks and balances to prevent the arbitrary use of governmental powers.[7]

Although a directly elected multi-party legislature exists, the electoral system has been designed in such a way as to include in the process only those groups which are not popularly and ideologically threatening to the leadership's secularist, evolutionary course of change and development. For example, the electoral laws are designed so as to ensure a huge majority for the ruling National Democratic Party (NDP) at the expense of independents and opposition parties. This has been the case with all the parliamentary elections held under President Mubarak. Not only did the 1984 election prove controversial, the opposition challenging it with charges of violence and forgery, leading Mubarak to dissolve the National Assembly in February 1987 and hold elections in April for a new one, these elections were also declared invalid, in 1990, by the Supreme Constitutional Court. A new electoral law was promulgated; it, too, was challenged on the ground that it made judicial supervision of elections a practical impossibility. Nevertheless, new elections were held in November 1990, albeit with low voter turnout, enabling the NDP to win an overwhelming majority of 348 out of 444 of the National Assembly's seats.[8]

The government's official rationale for all this was to avoid the rise of political extremism and too much fragmentation in the National Assembly, and thus to encourage development of a stable party system. However, it was also this provision that the Mubarak regime deployed to keep its most vocal and potentially powerful opponents, especially the radical Islamists, out of the process. It feared the reversal of fortunes that a possible electoral success of the Islamists could bring to its hold on power, and to the direction that it charted out for Egypt. This produced a growing polarization of the population along belligerent lines between Islamists, semi-secularists and secularists.

Although in relation to the subsequent People's Assembly elections in 1995 and 2000, the government found it expedient to agree to some changes in the electoral law, and allowed the 2000 elections to take place under full judicial supervision, Egyptian human rights groups raised serious concerns about the fairness of the elections. They reported numerous irregularities before and during the elections, 'including harassment, intimidation or often arrest of opposition candidates, the presence of security officials inside the polling stations, strong-arm tactics, designed to influence voting, and vote rigging'.[9] The Mubarak regime has continued to restrict freedom of association and expression: political parties cannot be formed without a licence from the government-controlled Political Parties Committee of the Shura Council. It has reserved the right to freeze or ban undesirable political groups and parties at whim, and execute arbitrary arrests of opponents under various penal codes on charges of slandering the leadership and/or the state, or working for foreign powers, as for example has been the case with the arrest and long-term sentencing in 2002 of a leading Egyptian sociologist and human rights campaigner and head of the Ibn Khaldun Center, Sa'adeddin Ibrahim.

As the Islamists have been able to thrive on mass poverty and on the regime's failure to procure marked improvement in the social and economic existence of the Egyptian masses, the regime has grown increasingly intolerant of Islamists, and has shown a great determination to suppress them by whatever means possible. It has pursued a two-pronged approach. On the one hand, it has sought to discredit Islamists by encouraging debate in the official media between different Islamic figures and groups and pitching them against one another, in order to highlight how divided they are among themselves, and how inept the radical Islamists would be if allowed to be major players in running the country. On the other, it has used maximum force whenever necessary against those Islamic elements and their supporters who have expressed open opposition to the regime, and whom it has labelled 'terrorists'.

This approach in many ways resembles that of the Shah, who branded his Islamic opponents either 'Islamic Marxists' or 'Islamic terrorists', making little attempt to open appropriate avenues of participation for them. The result has been a bloody struggle, which has cost many lives. With radical elements among the Islamists determined to achieve power through a campaign of violence designed to terrorize their opponents into submission, and the holders of power determined to maintain the status quo as the best way to preserve what is good for them, Egypt, a pivotal force in the Arab world, faces a future full of uncertainties.

The Algerian crisis also stems essentially from a decision by the ruling party to engage in a degree of democratization, but accept its outcome only on its terms. The National Liberation Front (FLN) had ruled Algeria single handedly since independence in 1962, instituting a one-party governmental system, and until the mid-1980s it persisted with a Soviet-type command approach to social and economic development. After seizing power through a military coup from the popular Ben Bella, who had led Algeria to independence, the FLN's military strong man, Houari Boumedienne, succeeded in transforming himself into an acceptable civilian leader, with a gift of political shrewdness and a knack for popular leadership. However, as time passed he tightened his grip on power through heavy reliance on the security and armed forces, and failed to manage the economy effectively, curb corruption within the ruling elite, or give a clear sense of direction and identity to Algerians. However, he benefited until his death in 1978 from close ties with the Soviet Union and its

East European allies, enabling him to maintain a degree of economic stability.

The situation changed with his successor, Colonel Chadli Bendjedid, who found himself not only with a mismanaged economy, growing political and social problems, and a revolt on the part of Algeria's Berber minority over legislation making Arabic the only official language, but also with dwindling Soviet support under Mikhail Gorbachev. Dissension became apparent within the FLN, social unrest broke out, and an Islamist opposition, which soon coalesced within the Islamic Salvation Front (FIS), scored well in local elections in 1987. The FLN's leadership found it expedient by the late 1980s to institute a number of constitutional reforms and some democratic measures, to improve the ruling party's popularity and thereby enhance its authority.[10]

The FLN, however, never felt that its rule had become so unpopular that its reforms would enable the very Islamic opponents that it wanted to marginalize to secure a major victory in the first round of fresh elections in 1991. The military abruptly cancelled the second round of elections due in January 1992, which FIS was poised to win. It imposed military rule, outlawed the FIS, and jailed many of its leaders in order to prevent the Islamic party from gaining power through the very electoral system that the FLN had devised. This plunged Algeria into a violent conflict, and dealt a severe blow to the cause of democratization in the Arab–Muslim world. The military's rationale was that if the Islamic party had been allowed to come to power, it would have imposed a theocratic rule similar to that of Iran, destroying the very democratic process which had brought it to power.[11] However, the real reason was that the FLN's leadership had devised the 'democratic' measures to strengthen its rule, not to give up power. It was prepared to make the system inclusive only as long as it constituted no danger to the FLN's political supremacy.

The military's reversal of the process may have brought a sigh of relief to many regimes in the region and the West, most importantly Egypt, France and the USA, which viewed the rise of FIS to power as threatening to their interests, but at the same time it drove the extremist elements within the FIS, some of them veterans of the Afghan Islamic resistance to Soviet occupation, to take up arms. The violence and repression that followed resulted in the death of over 100 000 Algerians in the 1990s, many of whom were slaughtered in unthinkably gruesome ways, and virtually paralysed Algeria as a functioning state. Moreover, it once again confirmed the crucial point that any system beyond veiled authoritarianism was not within easy reach in the Middle East.

When Bendjedid resigned under pressure, the military installed a former independence leader, Mohammed Boudiaf, in his place, but the new president was assassinated in June 1992. He was succeeded by another military backed leader, Ali Kalfa, until in early 1994, General Liamine Zeroual took over for a longer period. Zeroual could neither achieve a negotiated settlement with the Islamist opposition, nor curb rampant corruption in the military and its civilian cohorts within the ruling oligarchy. Finally, as a way out of the crisis, the military decided to hold presidential elections in April 1999. The opposition candidates withdrew from the race before the vote, amid claims of ballot rigging; the military's candidate, former foreign minister Abdelaziz Bouteflika, won the elections.

Bouteflika has certainly succeeded, through a policy of cooptation and repression, in bringing the level of violence down, but has not been able to address the fundamental causes of the crisis, nor has his regime been able to move beyond veiled authoritarianism. In many ways, Algeria is in a holding pattern.

If one glances across the domain of Islam as a whole, it becomes apparent that the problems and complexities which have confronted Iran, Egypt and Algeria in the process of democratization apply to most other Muslim countries as well. With reference to the Muslim Arab world alone, the UNDP's *Arab Human Development Report 2002* notes:

There is a substantial lag between Arab countries and other regions in terms of participatory governance. The wave of democracy, that transformed governance in most of Latin America and East Asia in the 1980s and Eastern Europe and much of Central Asia in the late 1980s and early 1990s, has barely reached the Arab states. This freedom deficit undermines human development and is one of the most painful manifestations of lagging political development. While *de jure* acceptance of democracy and human rights is enshrined in constitutions, legal codes and government pronouncements, *de facto* implementation is often neglected and, in some cases, deliberately disregarded. In most cases, the governance pattern is characterized by a powerful executive branch that exerts significant control over all other branches of the state, being in some cases free from institutional checks and balances. Representative democracy is not always genuine and sometimes absent. Freedoms of expression and association are frequently curtailed. Obsolete norms of legitimacy prevail.[12]

What has transpired in most Muslim countries is an *arbitrary* system of government, resting very much on the operation of an array of intelligence services (*mukhaberat*) under the direct control of the ruler, in violation of the very basic principles of the rule of law, separation of powers and independent judiciary. Concentration of too much arbitrary and innovative power in the hands of state leaders has enabled these leaders not only to act at whim in the sphere of politics, but also to interfere too much in the realms of economics and culture to meet political needs. This has led to failure to 'adapt to demands of the new economics and the new politics' effectively and efficiently. In most of the oil-rich Arab states, oil wealth is treated very much as the property of the rulers, and the income from it is dispensed in such manner, with few processes or mechanisms in place to ensure responsibility, accountability or transparency. Modernization and infrastructural development have certainly been given high priority in these countries, but little attempt has been made to link their past to the present and future, and thus avoid the usual problem of identity confusion which arises from lack of clear direction in abrogation of the past. In the oil-rich states, especially Saudi Arabia and its GCC partners, it is more the culture of shopping-centre consumerism, waste and lost opportunities that has gripped the citizens, rather than the culture of individual self-fulfillment through creative education and art, and critical self-assessment. In the poor Muslim countries, it is the culture of day-to-day economic survival that mainly preoccupies most citizens.

In most Muslim states, these disparities are coupled with numerous other associated social, cultural and economic problems. Despite some improvement in women's education, gender inequality remains rampant. 'The utilisation of Arab women's capabilities through political and economic participation remains the lowest in the world'.[13] Women have by and large been shackled by cultural norms and practices which have prevented them from making the contributions that they could to the construction and running of their societies. Most of these norms and practices are rooted in outdated cultural traditions and enforced by a patriarchal mode of behaviour rather than by

Islam. They are not uniformly spread in the Muslim world, but vary from country to country. The gender disparities are further exacerbated by low-quality education, from which most of the Muslim countries suffer. Constrained by politics and custom, education in most of these countries puts more emphasis on uncritical thinking than on creative learning and research. There is scarcely a single world-class university anywhere in the Muslim world. The tradition of memorization and blind indoctrination continues to constitute an obstacle to creative scholarly inquiry. This has created a critical 'knowledge gap', which in turn has affected all other fields of human activities in a majority of Muslim states.

In addition, the demographic structures in most Muslim countries are such that young people below the age of 25 form more than 50 per cent of the population. In most of the oil-rich states, many young high school and university graduates are underutilized, either because they are rich and need not work, or because the governments have limited the opportunities for them, preferring for most non-managerial areas to engage expatriates, who, if they engage in trade union activities or make demands on the government, can, unlike citizens, easily be deported. This has generated a gentry class, many members of which have little to keep them occupied and plenty of time to reflect on their circumstances beyond the need of being loyal and constructive citizens. The reverse of this situation prevails in poorer Muslim states; there, weak economies and widespread inequality and poverty prevail, and unemployment and under-employment, especially among young people, are rampant. Yet the two different situations have both generated endemic social problems, with many frustrated young people lacking direction or purpose in life. It is important to note that even in the case of better-off Arab components of the Muslim domain, 'GDP in all Arab countries combined stood at $531.2 billion in 1999 – less than that of a single European country, Spain ($595.5 billion)'.[14]

One of the central outcomes relevant to this study is that at least in most of the Arab countries, there is a 'mismatch between aspirations and their fulfillment', as well as 'alienation and its offspring – apathy and discontent'.[15] Given the lack of democratic principles of government, the alienation has created serious legitimation problems for the rulers and their governmental systems, with which the people have found it increasingly difficult to identify. It has also reflected a high level of distrust, not only between rulers and ruled, but also among the people themselves. This factor played an important role in the overthrow of the Shah, and has contributed, especially in the context of wider exogenous factors, ranging from Israel's repression of the Palestinians and the USA's support for Israel to the USA's dominance in the Middle East and preeminence since September 11, 2001 in Central Asia, to widespread disillusionment across the domain of Islam. By the same token, it has provided fertile ground for recruitment by radical Islamists such as Bin Laden and his Al Qaeda network, and for exploitation by secularist militants such as Saddam Hussein.

The Roots of Authoritarianism

A variety of national and crossnational reasons can be cited to explain why most of the Arab–Muslim world has proved so inhospitable to anything more than veiled authoritarianism. At least five in the literature are worthy of particular attention.

The first is the degree of incompatibility that allegedly exists between Islam and competitive pluralist democracy. It is argued that Islam, with its central principle of *Tawhid*, from which other Islamic principles flow, including those concerning earthly governance – most importantly the principles of *Shura* (consultation) and *Ijma* (consensus) – essentially provides for little more than what Mawlana Mawdudi has called 'theo-democracy';[16] and is therefore a foundation for an authoritarian, not liberal, political culture. Consequently, what has happened in the Muslim world since the Golden Age of Islam – the period of the Prophet Mohammed's and his Companions' rule – has been incremental acculturation of the masses by authoritarian values and practices, although with variations in their intensity and effectiveness from time to time and place to place.[17] This phenomenon took a sharper upward turn following the closure of the gate of *ijtihad*. Having said this, there is also the counter-argument, advanced by such thinkers and activists as Mohammed Khatami and Abdurrahman Wahid, that essentially Islam is compatible with democracy, and it all depends on how Islam is interpreted and applied. If one goes down a traditionalist path, as neofundamentalists and many radical Islamists do, Islam can be cited to negate some of the liberal principles of democracy related to individualism and freedom of choice. On the other hand, this need not be the case, provided one applies Islam through an *ijtihadi* approach according to changing times and conditions.

The second factor, which in many ways flows from the first, is that personalization, as against institutionalization, of politics has become deeply entrenched in the Arab world in particular, and in the Muslim world in general. Many date the origins of this back to the leadership of the Prophet, when the force of personality, not necessarily the force of political institutions, provided for political stability and continuity. The patriarchal nature of Arab societies, predating Islam, has simply contributed to and been strengthened by this factor. Although the Prophet was full of benevolence, his example of political leadership has not always been emulated rightly in the Muslim domain since the Golden Age. With rulership frequently falling into the hands of self-seeking and self-centred individuals, families, clans and elites, the need for institutionalization of politics has grown more acute than ever.

The third factor cited is the public's lack of sufficient understanding to enable it easily to grasp the significance of democratic values, with responsibility and crosscultural understanding and commitment. The forces of authoritarian exclusivism and the culture of divisiveness and distrust that it has generated have substantially thwarted the growth of liberal education, and therefore the degree of intellectual diversity and free discourse which are so vital for the innovative, pluralist development of societies.

The fourth factor concerns the lack of consensus over the form and functions of government, a problem which has historically dogged most of the countries in the Muslim world. Few Arab or non-Arab Muslim states have so far succeeded in fostering, as against imposing, a viable national approach to, and agreement on, what constitutes good and acceptable government. Although the Islamic regime in Iran put this issue to the people in a referendum in 1979, the fact that it was done without the provision of any alternative greatly reduced its significance.

The fifth factor is related to the effects of European colonial domination and then the USA's globalist penetration and hegemonic interventions in the domain of Islam. In general, European colonization did little to promote the cause of good government and principles of human rights and responsibilities. British colonial rule proved more rewarding in terms of the judicial and institutional legacy that it left behind in the Indian subcontinent than in the Muslim realm.

A survey of the colonial subjugation of Muslim lands clearly indicates that the colonial powers, whether British, French, Spanish, Dutch or Italian, paid far less attention to the task of nation-building and institutionalization of politics in their Muslim colonies than the British perhaps did in the subcontinent. The only place that may have proved an exception is the British colony of Malaya. Otherwise, the history of European colonialism displays an attitude of divide and rule, and exploitation of the Muslim colonies for whatever they were worth. A sense of cultural superiority formed part of this attitude. The colonial powers made little effort to take the future well-being of their Muslim subjects into consideration in ruling them. In most cases, they deliberately thwarted the need for good governance in order to facilitate maintenance of their domination. When French and British colonial rule of the Muslim Middle East finally folded up, with the partial exception of Egypt, little had been achieved in terms of political institutions and practices that could promote democracy. The postcolonial governments were confronted with the difficult task of starting nation-building from scratch, and leading their citizens from the colonial political culture to a new one.

Yet this was not all. In their transition, they now had to contend with another development: US globalist behaviour in the context of the Cold War. As was explained in Chapter 3, the US approach was overarching; it made no bones about what type of leader, government or sub-national force the USA dealt with, as long as it was prepared to support the USA's top foreign policy goal of containing Soviet communism. In the process, it made little or no effort to tie its penetration of many key Muslim states to promotion of good governance and democracy. On the contrary, in several instances the USA actively propped up anti-communist dictatorial regimes, such as Saudi Arabia under King Abdul Aziz and his heirs, Iran under the Shah and Pakistan under civilian and military rulers from Ali Jinnah to General Mohammed Ayub Khan to General Zia ul-Haq. It pursued this approach throughout the Cold War and even afterwards, backing authoritarian or veiled authoritarian regimes in most other Muslim Middle East states, including post-Nasser Egypt, as well as post-Sukarno Indonesia. It was even prepared to court Saddam Hussein's dictatorship in order to compensate for the loss of the Shah's autocratic rule in Iran. Rarely did the USA seriously link its friendship or alliance with these states to the need for democratization and development of responsible, accountable and transparent governmental systems. In the wake of the Gulf War in 1991, President George Bush declared democratization as one of the US goals in the Middle East, but by the turn of the twenty-first century, the USA had very little to show for it; it remained committed to the same regimes from whose presence it had benefited over a long period of time. In fact, many analysts came to view Washington's stand as more supportive of dictatorship than democracy, as it could more easily maintain its dominance and protect its interests through dictatorial regimes in the region.

Democratization or Civil Society?

The lack of progress beyond veiled authoritarianism in most of the domain of Islam underscores a vital point: the necessary conditions either for cutting through or for leap-frogging authoritarianism are still out of reach in most Muslim countries. The way forward perhaps is not to press for immediate democratization of political systems, which would require profound changes in the power structures, with profound effects on the fortunes of the very leaderships which are expected to bring about these changes. The objective should be to prepare the conditions for good government and a civil society. Such government and society do not need to be in conformity with the exact institutional models which underpin the operation of governments and societies in the West. Methods and mechanisms would have to be founded on those ideals and practices that are conducive to the development of a virtuous polity, the creation of which is, after all, a central focus of Islam. The starting point would not necessarily be to call for a change of leadership, but to convince the leadership of the need to move towards such practices as separation of state and economy, separation of powers, institution of an independent judiciary, and critically, establishment of the rule of law, with an emphasis on legal free space for the life of the individual, protection against arbitrary arrest or imprisonment, and the inviolability of basic human rights and freedoms, as was to some extent the case with the Italian city states and even the Ottoman despotism. The risk, of course, is that the Islamic *sharia* may be seized on as a code on the basis of which neofundamentalists seek to establish a new autocracy, as did the Taliban in Afghanistan.

It is possible to achieve liberty – in terms of lessening the state's grip over society – without having Western-type democratic institutions first in place. However, the achievement of liberty could well open the way for democracy. Despite the prevalence of political authoritarianism, many practices pertinent to the development of civil society have already found their way into most of the countries in the Muslim world. An encouraging debate on such issues as the vitality of free market reform or liberalization of capital, public representation in governmental processes and wider space for individual innovations and personal freedoms has gained strength. Certain leaderships, whether willingly or for reasons of expediency, have been shown to have benefited from such a debate, and have taken steps to enhance foundations for the growth of civil society. What is needed is to build on these bases. But this cannot be achieved as long as the Muslim countries function in an international system where Islam is vilified and the world's only superpower keeps attaching primacy to the threat or use of 'overwhelming force' to solve problems that are essentially political in nature in world politics, and holds a veto power over Muslim countries according to its globalist interests.

Despite all their ugliness, the events of September 11 have injected a new life into the debate which had already started about the ways and means by which political liberalization can be achieved within the framework of promoting civil society, separation of powers, rule of law, and an independent judiciary as foundations for building democracy in the Muslim domain. Democracy is something which has emerged from the grassroots, and this in the Muslim world cannot be done independently of Islam, given its dominance in the life of Muslims; it has to be achieved in conjunction with Islam. In this context, Khatami's experiment in Iran may prove very important, and deserves to be given a chance and encouragement. Al-Farabi's *al-medina al-jama'iyya* (the democratic or the most admirable and happy city) should be the objective, not a crude replication of democracy as it exists in the USA or one of its democratic allies.

6

Conclusion: The Way Forward

The cataclysm of September 11 should not be viewed through a single frame. It did not take place in a vacuum. Nor were the terrorist attacks executed by a group which acted in isolation from deeply ingrained grievances that have gripped many across the Muslim world. Bin Laden and his Al Qaeda activists acted against the backdrop of cumulative, widespread disillusionment among Muslims with their ruling elites and conditions of political and social existence, and with the USA and its allies for their historically often contradictory and insensitive treatment of various parts of the domain of Islam. In other words, their terrorist actions were rooted in causes and conditions in whose generation the West in general, and the USA in particular, had played an important role, although not with consciously malign intent. In the war on terror, the USA and its allies have primarily focused on symptoms of terrorism rather than its root causes. What emanated from Afghanistan in the form of the Pakistan-allied Al Qaeda–Taliban terror was, by and large, symptomatic of a particular set of crossnational conditions in the Muslim world. The USA and its supporters cannot succeed in achieving their anti-terror objectives by use of force alone: they must move rapidly to tackle the very causes and conditions that enabled Al Qaeda to build a multinational network of activists (including some Western collaborators) that secured structural support from the Taliban and their Pakistani backers. The destruction of Al Qaeda and the Taliban will do little to eradicate terrorism waged in the name of Islam. It can only bring a temporary relief. As long as the conditions on which anti-Western Islamic radicalism can flourish remain unaddressed, more groups similar to Al Qaeda may emerge in the future. The US 'power' approach to the problem has certainly had some short-term

129

success: it has resulted in the dislodging of the Taliban and the fragmenting of Al Qaeda in Afghanistan. It has also put pressure on the Abu Sayyaf group in the Philippines and Jamaah Islamiyah in Indonesia, which *are* known to have had links with Al Qaeda, and some alleged Al Qaeda cells in the Caucasus and elsewhere. Further, it enabled the Bush Administration to up the ante on Saddam Hussein to secure his removal from power, although no connection has been established between the Iraqi regime and Al Qaeda's operations. But beyond this, it cannot be expected to be a viable means of addressing the political and social causes of international terrorism.

What is needed is a sound, elaborate, political strategy to tackle effectively those causal problems which are essentially political in nature and defy the use of military power as a means to resolving them, and to eliminate the sources of popular moral and political nourishment for those forces of political Islam that employ extremism as an instrument to settle their differences with the USA and its allies. This strategy needs to be formulated on the basis of multilateralism rather than unilateralism as the principle guiding relations between states in the international system. It has to be premised on an awareness that the USA will not succeed in fighting terrorism or in widening and safeguarding its interests in the Muslim world on a long-term basis unless it behaves in a way that wins the minds and hearts of the Muslim people. For too long, the USA has supported political and ideological causes and backed authoritarian regimes in Muslim countries which have brought misery, degradation and humiliation to many across the Muslim domain. It has done so while knowing that in most cases the causes have been essentially unjust, as in relation to Israel's continued repressive occupation of Palestinian lands. It has sustained regimes that have not represented the longing and aspirations of the people over whom they have ruled. The USA cannot disclaim responsibility for imposing the Shah's rule on the Iranian people, protecting theocracy in Saudi Arabia and supporting Mubarak's authoritarian regime in Egypt, playing a critical role in the demise of Sukarno, and allying with General Zia ul-Haq's dictatorship, just to mention a few.

The USA and its allies have to recognize that no matter what they think of Islam and its ways, this religion is, and will continue to be, the dominant force in the lives of over a billion Muslims, and that Islam has always served, as it will in the future, as a potent ideology in shaping the identity of its followers and in guiding them in resistance, liberation, reassertion and reform. As the democratic Islamist and human rights activist Rachid Ghannouchi argues, it is time for the world powers to come to terms with Islam. Commenting on the wave of Islamic resurgence in the last quarter of the twentieth century, he argues that 'Islam has come back to restore dignity to its followers, to liberate them from despotism, to regain the *Ummah*'s usurped legitimacy, to restrict the powers of the state, and to establish and reinforce the power of the people, the power of civil society'.[1] In a similar vein, Riaz Hassan concludes, in his empirical study of a number of Muslim countries, that there is

> robust evidence of strong religious commitment among a majority of Muslims from all walks of life. This commitment is grounded in the traditions of scriptural Islam and occupies a prominent place in the daily lives of the majority of Muslims, influencing their everyday activities. The evidence also shows that religious piety is socially constructed. This social construction is influenced by global and societal conditions. At the global level, the hegemonic cultural patterns of the West appear to provoke strong resistance in Muslim populations which expresses itself in the reassertion of Islamic identity, which in turn reinforces cultural pride and self-esteem as well as consciousness of an Islamic history which once bore the signature of superior cultural tradition.[2]

This means that, in their approach to the Muslim world, the USA and its allies should not only exercise a clear understanding of what Islam is all about and of the complex hold that this religion has on its adherents, but also take note of the fact that the more they pressure Muslims to mould them according to Western ways and interests, the more they are likely to risk generating resentment and resistance from Muslims. They should deal with Muslims in ways governed not by a sense of Western superiority, but rather by the need for mutual accommodation and principles of reciprocity. No one doubts that the USA, with or without its allies, has grown to be the world's most powerful actor, capable of shaping and reshaping the destiny of many nations as well as the world order as a whole. Muslims recognize this, but at the same time they expect the USA to exercise its power with an acute sense of justice and constructive responsibility. They could be forgiven for thinking that when the Muslims during their imperial days had the world under their feet, they rarely ventured beyond their religious dictates to cause havoc for Christians and Jews or to seek forcefully to make and remake them in their images. Yet since the rise of the European powers and US superpower, these actors have forcefully sought many times to shape and reshape the Muslim domain according to their interests. It must be disturbing to most Muslims to learn that now, once again, the USA under President Bush, backed by the United Kingdom, wants to be in a position to remake at least the Middle East and Central Asian components of the Muslim domain. A US invasion and occupation of Iraq for such a purpose risks widespread resentment and anger across the Muslim domain. It could cause a majority of Muslims to feel that the Bush Administration (which many believe has been too open to influence by the forces of Christian Right and pro-Israeli neoconservatives) and its allies are definitely out to pursue an agenda well beyond combating international terrorism – namely to secure a geopolitical marginalization of political Islam and to restructure Central Asia and the Middle East from Afghanistan to Morocco. The purpose is to ensure that never again can a force, whether religious or secular, be able to achieve a position whereby it could challenge US dominance in the region or threaten the interests of Israel. As the history of relations between the two sides has shown, such an attempt could only sow more seeds of distrust and hostility among Muslims towards the West. These seeds may not have immediate effects, but they could, as in the past, germinate in the long run to ensure eruption of more tension and conflict between future Muslim and Western generations.

Some scholars in the West, such as Bernard Lewis, Daniel Pipes and like-minded pro-Israeli scholars and policy makers, argue that the reason Bin Laden and his supporters were able to hit the USA directly and target its interests elsewhere was because the USA and its allies had failed to act decisively against them and other militant Islamic groups over their previous anti-US terrorist actions. They assert that there is now a need for the USA to make use of its military might and act resolutely against them as the best way to put an end to anti-US Islamic militancy.[3] They tend to uphold the view that the use of might rather than recourse to reason and justice is the best means to uproot the causes of terror, even if those causes have been founded on deeply ingrained injustices. The problem with this approach is that it has rarely paid off in history; it has done little in the long run to stop acts of retaliation, hostility and bloodshed, especially when there exists a host of popular grievances on which people can draw to take up the cause of those who have committed the acts of terror.

Unfortunately it is the primacy of the use of force above everything else that appears to have gripped President Bush and his neoconservative advisors in dealing with the political and social causes of Al Qaeda terrorism. They seem to be convinced, though erroneously, that the more hard power they can apply, the more positive results they will be able to secure in the long run. This also partly explains why the Bush Administration has persistently failed to be precise about what it means by international terrorism, or when an act of violence, whether perpetrated by a state or a sub-national group against innocent people for political purposes, becomes an act of terror. This has allowed his Administration's policy behaviour to be determined by what the former US President Jimmy Carter has called 'a core group of conservatives trying to realize long-pent-up ambitions under the cover of the proclaimed war against terrorism'.[4] It has also enabled those who have usurped either democracy, such as Pakistan's General Musharraf, or challenged the rights of others to resist repression and occupation, as in the case of Israeli Prime Minister Sharon, to use or even hijack the US war on terror for their purposes.

President Bush has equally been ambivalent as to what role he envisions for the USA in the countries where he seeks regime change and which need to be stabilized as part of a condition for the success of the USA's war on terror. Does he want the USA to act as 'an above the horizon' actor, that is, to secure enough bases and pre-positioned military hardware in Central Asia and the Middle East to take action militarily whenever necessary to deal with challenges as they arise? Or does he want the USA to go beyond this to get involved in the difficult task of nation-building to prevent such challenges from arising in the first place, and to promote the principles of freedom, democracy, justice and human development as necessary foundations for national and international stability. Since the September 11 events, he has vacillated between the two, but with a strong emphasis on the first. He has procured regime change in Afghanistan, with something of a commitment to nation-building in that country, and has sought to promote a similar process in Iraq. Yet at the same time, he has repeatedly expressed an aversion to nation-building – something which he has preferred the USA's European, Japanese, Australian and New Zealand allies to undertake. These ambiguities have caused much confusion around the world about what it is that ultimately the USA wants to achieve and what role it wants to play in achieving it. This confusion has gained potency even among those US allies that gave the Bush Administration unqualified support following the September 11 attacks.[5] This is one reason why most of the USA's main anti-terror coalition partners, especially at the level of the UN Security Council – that is France, Russia and China – have in the recent past refused to give the Bush Administration a *carte blanche* to take military action against Iraq in order to replace Saddam Hussein's regime with a palatable one, despite the repressive nature of the regime.

The September 11 tragedy certainly has confronted the USA and its allies, and the Muslim world with serious challenges. But the future of relations between the two sides will depend on whether they can turn these challenges into valuable opportunities to learn from the mistakes of the past, and build bridges of understanding based on common human values and interests of the kind that helped them to enjoy extended periods of positively interactive peaceful coexistence. There are plenty of reasoned and informed citizens in the West, and moderate Islamists and ordinary Muslims in the domain of Islam, who long for this development. For too long, the radical and neofundamentalist Islamists have been able to drown out the voices of moderate Islamists and many concerned ordinary Muslims in the Muslim world, and ideological zealots in the West have succeeded in drawing on their Islamist counterparts' radicalism to justify their own extremism and to create an atmosphere of distrust and hostility in the relations between the two sides. The time has come for civil society aspirants and activists from both sides of the divide to rise to the occasion not only to reach out to and engage one another, but also to deprive extremists, whether of religious or political-ideological nature, of the necessary space to pursue their extremist agendas.

There is a need for a shift in attitude and priorities in both the USA and its allies, and the Muslim world, and this certainly calls for wiser leadership and concomitant political changes in the West, more importantly the USA, and in the domain of Islam. In the case of the latter, it may even demand leadership changes from within in opposition to the existing authoritarian or veiled authoritarian arrangements which have bedevilled most Muslim countries and which have deprived them of the necessary opportunities to achieve a position whereby the USA and its allies will have no choice but to interact with them on the basis of principles of mutual respect and accommodation.

However, given the current tense atmosphere in which Washington's power play figures dominantly and the Muslims are subjected, wittingly or unwittingly, to this power play everywhere, the onus falls on the USA and its allies to change course to the extent necessary to allow not only their own civil society activists, but also those of the Muslim world, to reach out to one another. The Muslims can only move in the direction of better understanding and reconciliation on two conditions: if the USA and its allies restructure their geopolitical interests to allow (and even help) the Muslims to achieve what they need to do domestically; *and if they recognize the fact that Islam is not there for them to make or remake according to their interests.* Islam is an integrative factor in the life of a majority of Muslims; it cannot be sponged out of both deliberation and formulation of changes that Muslim societies have to undergo. Whether it is in relation to Iran or Algeria or Sudan, or for that matter any other Muslim country, the US government and its allies must not immediately panic when Islamic forces emerge to play a critical role in the process of change, as long as that process is popular, participatory and pluralist in nature and implementation. They should allow the process to take its course, even if it results in the rise to power of an Islamist group or party, for once that group or party assumes office, sooner or later it has to come to terms with the limitations of that office.

No example is more illustrative of this point than that of Iran. Despite all the determination by the Islamic hardline followers of Ayatollah Khomeini to remain in control of instrumentalities of state power, the face of the Iranian Islamic regime has substantially changed from its early days. Iran now enjoys a reasonable degree of political pluralism and participatory politics. Under President Khatami, the principles of the rule of law, separation of powers and certain human rights, including freedom of expression and immunity against arbitrary arrest, have gradually begun to make an imprint, with voters having a role in scrutinising the government's policies and actions. This is more so now than at any other time in Iran's history, with the exception of a brief period during Dr Mohammed Mossadeq's reformist government in the early 1950s, which was brought to an end by the CIA's successful covert operations in support of the Shah's dictatorship as discussed in Chapter 4. The Iranians have achieved all this over two decades after freeing themselves from the Shah's rule and US control. No one claims that Iran is a perfect democracy, free of many problems characterizing transitional societies; far from it. But it has undeniably achieved a more robust electoral and participatory system of government than any of its Arab counterparts. Similarly, if France had not backed, and the USA had not remained conspicuously silent on, the Algerian military's cancellation of the February 1992 elections, which the moderate Islamist FIS was set to win, Algeria may not have been plunged into the bloodbath that followed the military's action. There was a reasonable chance that a FIS regime would have evolved in a direction similar to that in which the Iranian Islamic regime has.

Democratic norms, values and practices are not something that can mushroom overnight; they take a long time to evolve, sometimes involving painful periods of political dislocation and civil disturbance, as the history of Western democracies have shown. The sad fact is that in the Muslim world, it is not just domestic factors but also exogenous actors that have thwarted the growth of popularly mandated, institutionalized systems of government and observance of human rights. Foreign powers, especially the USA since the end of the Second World War, found it both easy and desirable to back and uphold traditionalist dictatorial regimes as the main mechanism for ensuring their dominance in many parts of the Muslim domain. They made little or no effort to make direct connection with forces of liberalism and democratization, whether from the religious or secular sides of politics, or to reach out to the populace in Muslim countries. Driven by the impulse of its own realpolitik interests, the USA rarely ventured to ascertain the position of people hostage to authoritarian governments in their own countries. US governments have consistently failed to take on board the findings of various independent academic studies calling for the need to understand the gulf which has been growing between the rulers and the ruled, and between citizens' expectations and fulfilment of those expectations, in many Muslim countries. The USA has persistently deferred to the needs of regime preservation in these countries, although various US leaders have expressed awareness of the lack of democracy as a source of much public dissatisfaction and volatility in the Muslim domain.

Tragically, there does not seem to be any change in prospect in Washington's attitude, even in 2003. If anything, in the wake of the war on terror, in many cases Washington has shown more willingness than ever to add more dictators to its list of allies. They include General Musharraf of Pakistan as well as the authoritarian leaderships – though varying in degree – of the Central Asian republics of Uzbekistan, Turkmenistan, Tajikistan, Kazakhstan and Kyrgyzstan, who are now America's friends and partners in the war against terrorism. General Musharraf not only was the architect of the Kargill confrontation with India in early 1999, which brought the two sides close to a nuclear confrontation, but also instigated a coup later that year which toppled the elected government of Prime Minister Nawaz Sharif and inaugurated yet another period of military rule in Pakistan's short but very turbulent history. More importantly, General Musharraf continued to back the Taliban, and therefore the militia's Al Qaeda allies, right up to the tragedy of September 11.

However, once he changed sides to save himself and his regime from US wrath, President Bush adopted him as a kind of long-lost friend, and by April 2002 backed him in a manifestly flawed referendum to secure another five-year presidential term and thus perpetuate the entrenchment of the military's role in Pakistani politics. Musharraf held a general parliamentary election in mid-October 2002. Although the election enabled a number of Islamic groups to band together to gain control of two provincial assemblies (in Northwest Frontier and Baluchistan Provinces) on the border with Afghanistan and close to one-third of the seats in the lower house of national parliament in a backlash against Musharraf's anti-Taliban and anti-Al Qaeda alliance with the USA, international observers declared the election to be fundamentally flawed.[6] It was designed primarily to marginalize the main political parties and ensure that the military remains the dominant force in politics.

The Musharraf leadership is not in a strong position to meet all its promises to Washington to stamp out Islamic extremism and bring about a 'genuine democracy' in Pakistan, and pursue a strict policy of non-interference towards Afghanistan and Indian-administered Kashmir. Its biggest problem is not the inability to articulate a sound foreign policy, but an internal environment that can easily frustrate Musharraf's domestic and foreign policy promises. His promises will fall flat unless he tackles their root causes effectively: the out-of-control behaviour of the ISI, which has been the main sponsor of political and religious extremism; the inability to institute long overdue structural social and economic reforms, and to retrench the deep seated role of the military in politics; and confusion over Pakistan's national identity – will it be an Islamic state or a secular state with an Islamic outlook? Irrespective of how much support Musharraf receives from Washington, he lacks the necessary credentials and resources to prevent either the Taliban and Al Qaeda activists from using Pakistan's territory to mount operations in Afghanistan or renegade military and ISI elements from helping these activists and Kashmiri militants. It is widely believed that as soon as the USA thins out its forces in Afghanistan, the ISI and an array of its extremist Islamic clients will be ready to enhance their crossborder activities in Afghanistan as well as in Kashmir. Meanwhile, as an economically virtually bankrupt, and politically and socially deeply divided realm, armed with nuclear weapons, Pakistan remains a potentially explosive state.

Unless the USA changes course to exert pressure on Musharraf to restore genuine accountability and transparency, address Pakistan's dire social-economic conditions, reduce its military expenditure which consumes more than 50 per cent of the annual budget,[7] and dismantle the country's nuclear arsenals, Pakistan appears to pose a greater danger to regional and international stability than Saddam Hussein's Iraq. Yet the Bush Administration seems to be in no mood to do anything that could help the people of Pakistan to achieve democracy and a better standard of living if it might undermine Musharraf's position as one of the USA's best allies against terror. Even so, sooner or later the USA will need to face a choice between backing Musharraf and what is needed to empower the people of Pakistan and to keep Pakistan at bay so that the Afghans secure a real opportunity to determine their future and rebuild their country free of Pakistan's military–ISI interference.

The Bush Administration likewise has been prompt to embrace the Central Asian republics and has been rewarded with access to air space and bases. With the exception to some extent of Kyrgyzstan, the regimes in all of these republics are authoritarian and led by what one can term 'recycled communists'. Their social and economic reforms are faltering, and the scope for public discontent, instability and Islamic challenges remains – to different degrees in the various republics – worrying. Although Islam's hold on Central Asian peoples is not as uniformly deep as is the case with neighbouring Afghanistan, Iran, Pakistan and beyond, political repression and socioeconomic disparities and low standards of living have led elements in some of these republics, especially Uzbekistan and Tajikistan, to embrace Islam as an ideology of opposition and reform. This, too, is bound to confront the USA with difficult choices and dilemmas: it will be a hard call on it to reconcile its support of dictatorships with the need for democratization as the best means to deter people from drifting towards Islamic radicalism in some of the republics.

It is important that the USA and its supporters should not conduct the war on terror with a mindset that insists that everything else be subordinated to the requirements of 'success' in this war, as they did in pursuit of containing and defeating Soviet communism during the first decades of the Cold War. The use of force has no utility when it comes to winning over those Muslims who distrust the USA and its allies, and their policy intentions and actions. The best way to win them over and undercut their reasons for gravitating towards extremism as a means to vent their frustrations and grievances is for the USA to join forces with the international community to work out a multilateral and cooperative strategy to create a more viable international environment in which the Muslims and the religion of Islam are not subjected to the kind of political pressure that plays into the hands of extremists from both sides. In immediate terms, the chances of generating such an environment will depend on the role that the USA and its allies will play in the outcome of a number of problematic issues within the domain of Islam.

The first is the rebuilding of Afghanistan, with a stable political order. Now that the rule of the Taliban has gone and Al Qaeda is on the run, it is imperative to do whatever it takes to achieve the intertwined goals of reconstruction, security and stability as rapidly as possible.[8] The USA and its allies, helped by a largely sympathetic international community, have taken the initial steps in this regard, but by the end of 2002 it was evident that they still had a very long way to go. The Karzai government had moved from interim to transitional position, with the task of paving the way for a democratically elected government before the middle of 2004, and the 5000-strong International Security Assistance Force (ISAF) had performed well in securing the Karzai government and Kabul. However, the political, security and reconstruction situation remained fragmented and fragile at the national level.[9] There was no noticeable improvement in the Afghans' living conditions to divert many of them from a culture of the gun to a culture of peace. The authorities and international humanitarian agencies struggled to cope with the return of nearly two million refugees over one year from neighbouring countries. The Afghan finance minister complained – justly – that the international community had not matched its words with deeds in relation to rebuilding Afghanistan. Of $4.5 billion reconstruction aid promised at the Tokyo donors' conference in January 2002, $1.8 billion of it to be disbursed during 2002, over $1 billion had been delivered before the end of year, with 80 per cent being spent on food and other humanitarian purposes rather than long-term reconstruction.

As international concern grew about the effects on US involvement in Afghanistan of a possible US military campaign to oust Saddam Hussein's regime in Iraq, some analysts were openly critical of the USA for failing to invest enough in Afghanistan's security and reconstruction.[10] The *Washington Post* claimed that the Bush Administration had underinvested in Afghan security and reconstruction and that as a result '[t]he influence and prestige of the central government in Kabul are steadily shrinking rather than growing, the countryside has become more and more dangerous, and even the capital is no longer safe'. It aptly concluded that 'Karzai's government cannot build its authority until it can begin to deliver the rebuilt roads, aqueducts and schools that average Afghans long for. Right now it does not have the money even to fund its meagre bureaucracy'.[11] Afghanistan has now reached a point in its post-Taliban transformation where any faltering in its political, economic and security reconstruction could easily lead it back to chaos and conflict – a development which would cost the USA the goodwill that it had earned among a majority of Afghans for ending the Taliban rule and dismantling the Al Qaeda network in the country.

The second issue is related to the situation in Pakistan and the Central Asian republics. In the wake of September 11, the USA managed to achieve unprecedented preeminence in these countries. But the question remains how and for what purpose the USA will use this preeminence: will it use it exclusively to hunt down Al Qaeda and advance its own global interests, or will it use it to benefit the people of the region and stabilize the area on a long-term basis? If it is the former, the USA will have little chance of helping to bring about the structural political, social and economic changes which are necessary to stimulate processes of democratization and improve conditions of living and prospects of long-term stability in any of the constituent states. Such structural changes are urgently needed if the USA and its allies are interested in deterring religious and secularist extremism from becoming an instrument of change or opposition in any of the region's countries, and in ensuring that Pakistan will not again become adventurous towards Afghanistan, and will secure the necessary domestic basis to settle with India for a viable resolution of Kashmir. Anything short of this could exacerbate the conditions for the region to languish in uncertainty and volatility, with a real threat to an unravelling of the USA's war on terror.

The third issue concerns the US attitude towards the Iranian Islamic regime. Although the Iranian situation, in which the minority Islamic hardliners still control most of the organs of state power while moderate Islamist reformers have the support of a great majority of the Iranian people, is far from satisfactory, it is imperative for the USA not to do anything which could inadvertently undermine the position of reformists. The latter have made steady progress in changing the nature of politics from the early years of the Iranian revolution, without risking a bloody confrontation with their factional opponents. Washington must recognize this and the fact that the process of creating a publicly mandated participatory system of governance with an assurance of basic human rights even within an Islamic form, as is the case in Iran, will take a long time, involving many ups and downs. It is better to have such a process with the prospect of eventually giving rise to a full fledged democracy than one which may be imported from outside with little chance of finding sufficient grassroots support. Washington will do well by its own interests and those of the Iranians to support this process and work towards a rapprochement with Tehran on this basis. Khatami's experiment deserves a chance to succeed, and if it comes off it may provide a model for a number of other Muslim countries.

The fourth issue is the Palestinian problem, which is in urgent need of a viable resolution. This problem has been a constant source of accumulated anti-US frustration and anger across the Arab and, for that matter, the Muslim worlds. Not only Bin Laden but many more like him can easily draw on this problem to recruit dedicated supporters and galvanize anti-US sentiment in the region, given the

USA's strategic partnership with Israel. Israel must be made to understand that ultimately its peace and security are intertwined with those of the Palestinians, and without a viable independent Palestinian state there can be no peace and security for Israel. A first step would be a clear break from the uncritical support that *any* Israeli leader can expect to receive from Washington, irrespective of his record or policies. The Palestinian issue has its own deeply rooted complexities: it is not just one peripheral aspect of the war against terrorism, and it is a grave error to link the two issues.

The fifth issue is Iraq. Saddam Hussein's regime is morally and politically indefensible and deserves to be disarmed of weapons of mass destruction. But Iraq's situation needs to be viewed against the backdrop of the British-administered, violent formation of the Iraqi state more than 50 years ago, and in the context of US support of Saddam Hussein's regime in the 1980s, as well as the consequences that a forced US removal of it from power might entail not only for Iraq and the region, but the Muslim world as a whole. A weapons of mass destruction (WMD) disarmament of Iraq is still achievable through a policy of stringent deterrence and containment, targeted in such a way as not to harm the Iraqi people. The USA has often claimed that this worked against the Soviet Union: why not against Saddam Hussein's regime? Alternatively, the best option is to achieve the objective through a regime of region-wide arms control, involving Israel, which possesses WMD but has deliberately been kept out of the loop by the USA. A disarmament of Iraq on its own will do little to prevent future leaders from emerging in the region with a determination to match Israel's capabilities. As for regime change, whether in Iraq or for that matter any other country, it will have to come about as a result of domestic changes and citizens' actions, not an outside power. Any attempt on the part of Washington to effect regime change without manifest justification is fated to rebound.

The sixth issue is that of democratization in the Arab world in particular, and in the domain of Islam in general. Here, what is needed is to foster the necessary conditions for development of the rule of civil society, the rule of law, the separation of powers, an independent judiciary, and human rights as solid foundations for liberalization and democratization of the polity in cooperation with those forces, whether belonging to the religious or secular sides of the political spectrum, which are dedicated to the goal of achieving such foundations. Regimes in most of the Muslim realm need, more than ever before, to widen public participation in both policy making and policy implementation arenas within pluralist, responsible and transparent governmental frameworks. A failure in this respect can only ensure the continuation of those popular political and social frustrations that make many people, especially the young, susceptible to Islamic radicalization. Political disillusionment is widespread, especially in the Arab world, and often it is this disillusionment that finds channels of expression through other causes, more importantly anti-Israeli and anti-US causes. As long as this remains the case, many more like Bin Laden or Saddam Hussein will find fertile ground on which to draw to defend their positions and galvanize public discontent against the USA and its allies.

Notes

1 September 11 and its Aftermath

1. For details of President Bush's measures in this respect, see 'President Bush's Proposal for Homeland Security', *Washington Post* (Homepage), 6 June 2002.
2. *Washington Post*, 11 June 2002.
3. For an excellent discussion, see Richard Falk, *Predatory Globalization* (Malden, MA: Polity Press, 1999).
4. Samuel P. Huntington, *The Clash of Civilizations and the Remaking of World Order* (London: Touchstone Books, 1998), p. 212.
5. Edward Said, 'Two Civilisations, Deeply Entwined', *The Age*, 23 October 2001.
6. George W. Bush, 'Address to a Joint Session of Congress and the American People', *New York Times*, 20 September 2001.
7. Zbigniew Brzezinski, 'Confronting Anti-American Grievances', *New York Times*, 1 September 2002.
8. ABC News, 5 September 2002.
9. United Nations Security Council, S/RES/1397 (12 March 2002).
10. *The Guardian*, 27 September 2001; *BBC World News*, 28 September 2001.
11. Raeed N. Tayeh, 'Members of Congress Send Letters to Ashcroft Regarding Offensive Comments about Islam', American Muslims for Global Peace and Justice, 8 April 2002, www.globalpeaceandjustice.org/prs/po04-29-02.htm.
12. For example, see Andrew Bolt, 'Holy War of Words', *Herald-Sun*, 30 May 2002, and Andrew Bolt, 'Giving Thanks Where Due', *Herald-Sun*, 3 June 2002.
13. Frank Newport, 'Gallup Poll of the Islamic World', http://www.gallup.com/poll/tb/goverPubli/20020226.asp?Version==p, 26 February 2002.

2 Shared Values and Conflicts: The Historical Experience

1. For various interpretations of Islam in the modern world, see James P. Piscatori, *Islam in a World of Nation-States* (Cambridge: Cambridge University Press, 1986), esp. ch. 1.
2. For a good discussion, see John L. Esposito, *Unholy War: Terror in the Name of Islam* (New York: Oxford University Press, 2002), ch. 2.
3. See Michael Walzer, *Just and Unjust Wars: A Moral Argument with Historical Illustrations* (New York: Basic Books, 1992).
4. For a detailed discussion, see Wael B. Hallaq, 'On the Origins of the Controversy about the existence of Mujtahids and the Gate of Ijtihad', *Studia Islamica*, 63 (1986), pp. 129–41.

5. Jonathan Bloom and Sheila Blair, *Islam: A Thousand Years of Faith and Power* (New Haven: Yale University Press, 2002), pp. 79–80.
6. Karen Armstrong, *Islam: A Short History* (New York: Modern Library, 2000), p. 132.
7. For details, see Alan Buchan Theobald, *The Mahdiya: A History of the Anglo-Egyptian Sudan, 1881–1899* (London: Longman, Green, 1951).
8. For a comprehensive discussion, see Nikki R. Keddie, *An Islamic Response to Imperialism: Political and Religious Writings of Sayyid Jamal al-Din 'al-Afghani'* (Berkeley and Los Angleles: University of California Press, 1968), Part 1.
9. Armstrong, *Islam: A Short History*, p. 156.
10. John L. Esposito, *The Islamic Threat: Myth or Reality?* (New York: Oxford University Press, 1992), pp. 120–4.
11. For Islamic reformation in Turkey, see Wilfred Cantwell Smith, *Islam in Modern History* (New York: Mentor, 1957), ch. 4.
12. Amin Saikal, 'Kemalism: Its Influences on Iran and Afghanistan', *International Journal of Turkish Studies*, 2:2 (1982–83), pp. 25–32.

3   US Globalism and Regional Domination

1. For a full discussion, see Harold Sprout and Margaret Sprout, *The Rise of American Naval Power, 1776–1918* (Princeton: Princeton University Press, 1946), chs 7–16.
2. For a detailed discussion, see Amin Saikal, *The Rise and Fall of the Shah* (Princeton: Princeton University Press, 1980), pp. 13–15.
3. *Foreign Relations of the United States, Diplomatic Papers: The British Commonwealth, the Near East and Africa* (Washington, DC: Government Printing Office, 1959), pp. 374–82.
4. George Lenczowski, *Russia and the West in Iran, 1918–1948: A Study in Big-Power Rivalry* (Ithaca: Cornell University Press, 1949), pp. 219–21.
5. For a detailed discussion of US–Saudi relations during this period, see Aaron David Miller, *Search for Security: Saudi Arabian Oil and American Foreign Policy, 1939–1949* (Chapel Hill: University of North Carolina Press, 1980).
6. Lord George Nathaniel Curzon, *Persia and the Persian Question*, vol. I, reprint (London: Frank Cass & Co., 1966), p. 3.
7. See *US State Department Bulletin*, 14:621 (28 May 1951), p. 851.
8. For American views, see *The New York Times*, 14 April 1947; *Congressional Record*, 93:5, p. 6341, 80th Congress, 1st Session, 4 June 1947, House; *Congressional Record*, Appendix, 93:12, p. 2968, 80th Congress, 1st Session, 19 June 1947, House.
9. *US State Department Bulletin*, 28 (9 February 1953), pp. 831–6.
10. Sejara Indonesia, '1950 to 1965: The Sukarno Years', http://www.gimonca. com/sejarah/sejarah09.html.
11. David Joel Steinberg *et al.*, *In Search of Southeast Asia* (London: Pall Mall Press, 1971), p. 400.

12. Amin Saikal, 'Soviet Policy Toward Southwest Asia', *The Annals of the American Academy of Political and Social Science*, 481 (September 1985), p. 106.

4   The Great Issues

* The latter part of this section and part of the first section of Chapter 5 are based on Amin Saikal, 'Peace and Democracy in Iran and Iraq', in Amin Saikal and Albrecht Schnabel (eds), *Democratization in the Middle East: Experiences, Struggles, Challenges* (Tokyo: United Nations University Press, 2003).

1. For details, see Dankwart A. Rustow and John F. Mugno, *OPEC: Success and Prospects* (New York: New York University Press, 1976), p. 131.
2. Amin Saikal, *The Rise and Fall of the Shah* (Princeton: Princeton University Press, 1980), pp. 207–8.
3. *The Age*, 9 August 1976.
4. *Sydney Morning Herald*, 17 November 1977.
5. Barry Rubin, 'The United States and Iraq: From Appeasement to War', in Amatzia Baram and Barry Rubin (eds), *Iraq's Road to War* (London: Macmillan, 1993), p. 255.
6. For the text of conversation between the members of the delegation and President Saddam Hussein, see Micah L. Siftry and Christopher Cerf (eds), *The Gulf War Reader: History, Documents, Opinion* (New York: Random House, 1991), pp. 119–21.
7. The Gulf Cooperation Council is composed of Saudi Arabia, Oman, United Arab Emirates, Kuwait, Bahrain and Qatar.
8. For a critical assessment of the Islamic regime, see Martin Wright, *Iran: The Khomeini Revolution* (Harlow, Essex: Longman, 1989), esp. pp. 31–42; Hazhir Teimourian, 'Iran's 15 Years of Islam', *The World Today*, 50:4 (April 1994), pp. 67–70; Darius M. Rejali, *Torture and Modernity: Self, Society, and State in Modern Iran* (Boulder: Westview Press, 1994), esp. chs 7–8.
9. For a detailed discussion of the concept of *jihad* in Islam, see Rudolph Peters (trans.), *Jihad in Medieval and Modern Islam: The Chapter on Jihad from Averroes' Legal Handbook 'Bidayat al-mudjtahid' and the Treatise 'Koran and Fighting' by the Late Shaykh-al-Azhar, Mahmud Shaltut* (Leiden: Brill, 1977).
10. For a discussion and different meanings of the concept, see Joseph Schacht, *The Origins of Muhammadan Jurisprudence* (Oxford: Clarendon Press, 1975); Wael B. Hallaq, 'Was the Gate of Ijtihad Closed', *International Journal of Middle East Studies*, 16 (1984), pp. 3–41; and Bernard G. Weiss, 'Interpretation in Islamic Law: The Theory of Ijtihad', *American Journal of Comparative Law*, 26 (Spring 1978), pp. 199–212.
11. For a discussion of Soroush's ideas, see Valla Vakili, *Debating Religion and Politics in Iran: The Political Thought of Abdulkarim Soroush*, Occasional Paper Series no. 2 (New York: Council on Foreign Relations, 1996).
12. Mohammad Khatami, 'Dialogue and the New Millennium', Address delivered to the 30th General Conference of the United Nations Educational, Scientific and Cultural Organization (UNESCO), Paris, 29 October 1999, p. 2.

13. Mohammad Khatami, *Islam, Dialogue and Civil Society* (Canberra: Centre for Arab and Islamic Studies, Australian National University, 2000), p. 111.
14. 'Statement by H.E. Seyyed Mohammad Khatami President of the Islamic Republic of Iran and Chairman of the Eighth Session of the Islamic Summit Conference Tehran, 9 December 1997', *Iranian Journal of International Affairs*, IX:4 (Winter 1997/98), p. 601.
15. Ibid., p. 603.
16. Khatami, *Islam, Dialogue and Civil Society*, pp. 53–4.
17. Ruhollah Khomeini, *Sahifey-e Noor* (The Book of Light) vol. 21 (Tehran: Markaz-e Madarek Anghlab-e Islami, 1990), p. 47.
18. Khatami, *Islam, Dialogue and Civil Society*, p. 57.
19. Ibid., p. 104.
20. Ibid., p. 85.
21. Ibid., p. 90.
22. John. F. Burns, 'Former Hanging Judge of Iran', *The New York Times*, 23 October 1999.
23. Zbigniew Brzezinski, Brent Scowcroft and Richard Murphy, 'Differentiated Containment', *Foreign Affairs*, 76:3 (May–June 1997), pp. 20–30.
24. *The Washington Post*, 11 August 2002.
25. For the perspective of a leading democrat Islamist, Rachid Ghannouchi, see Azzam S. Tamimi, *Rachid Ghannouchi: A Democrat Within Islamism* (New York: Oxford University Press, 2001), pp. 178–80.
26. For details and breakdown of grants and loans, see Clyde R. Mark, 'Israel: US Foreign Assistance', *Issue Brief for Congress* (Washington, DC: Congressional Research Service, 6 June 2002); and Camille Mansour, *Beyond Alliance: Israel in US Foreign Policy* (New York: Columbia University Press, 1994), p. 190.
27. *Washington Report on Middle East Affairs*, August/September 1996, p. 104.
28. For statistical data about Israel's rate of economic growth and military strength see, *Statistical Yearbook 1993* (New York: United Nations, 1995), p. 160; and *The Military Balance, 1994–1995* (London: International Institute for Strategic Studies, 1995), pp. 132–3.
29. Ze'ev Schiff and Ehud Ya'ari, *Intifada: The Palestinian Uprising – Israel's Third Front*, trans. Ina Freedman (New York: Simon & Schuster, 1990), p. 237.
30. For a good discussion of Hamas's organization and operations, see Giles Kepel, *Jihad: The Trail of Political Islam*, trans. Anthony F. Roberts (Cambridge, MA: Belknap Press of Harvard University Press, 2002), ch. 14.
31. Amin Saikal and William Maley, *Regime Change in Afghanistan: Foreign Intervention and the Politics of Legitimacy* (Boulder: Westview Press, 1991), ch. 5.
32. For details, see John K. Cooley, *Unholy Wars: Afghanistan, America and International Terrorism* (London: Pluto Press, 1999), ch. 5.
33. For a detailed discussion of this issue and America's operations in Pakistan and beyond, although containing some factual inaccuracies, see Cooley, *Unholy Wars*, esp. chs 3, 5 and 9.
34. Amin Saikal, 'Afghanistan's Ethnic Conflict', *Survival*, 40:2 (Summer 1998), pp. 116–18.

35. Cited in William Maley, *The Afghanistan Wars* (London: Palgrave Macmillan, 2002), p. 254.
36. A detailed account of US–Bin Laden interplay is given in Cooley, *Unholy Wars*, ch. 10.
37. For a detailed discussion of Bin Laden's life and views, as well as the structure, ideology and operations of Al Qaeda, see Rohan Gunaratna, *Inside Al Qaeda: Global Network of Terror* (London: Hurst, 2002), esp. chs 1–2.
38. For details, see Rafael Reuveny and Aseem Parkash, 'The Afghanistan War and the Breakdown of the Soviet Union', *Review of International Studies*, 25:4 (1999), pp. 693–708.
39. William Maley, 'Interpreting the Taliban', in William Maley (ed.), *Fundamentalism Reborn? Afghanistan and the Taliban* (London: Hurst, 1998), pp. 1–28.
40. For details, see Ahmed Rashid, *Taliban: Militant Islam, Oil and Fundamentalism in Central Asia* (New Haven: Yale Nota Bene, Yale University Press, 2000).
41. For good discussions of Pakistan's relations with the Taliban and America's role in it, see Ahmed Rashid, 'Pakistan and the Taliban', and Richard Mackenzie, 'The United States and the Taliban', both in Maley (ed.), *Fundamentalism Reborn?*, pp. 72–89, 90–103.
42. For a detailed discussion, see Saikal, 'Afghanistan's Ethnic Conflict', p. 119.
43. *Reuters*, 18 November 1997, and *Voice of America*, 18 November 1997.

5 Democracy and Authoritarianism

1. For details, see Alexis de Tocqueville, *Democracy in America*, ed. and abr. by Richard D. Heffner (New York: Mentor, 1956).
2. Anthony Arblaster, *Democracy* (Milton Keynes: Open University Press, 1987), p. 8.
3. For a discussion of different models of democracy, see David Held, 'Democracy: From City-states to a Cosmopolitan Order', *Political Studies*, XL: Special Issue (1992), pp. 10–39.
4. Amin Saikal, *The Rise and Fall of the Shah* (Princeton: Princeton University Press, 1980), ch. 8.
5. For details, see Said Amir Arjomand, *The Turban for the Crown: The Islamic Revolution in Iran* (New York: Oxford University Press, 1988), esp. ch. 8; Amin Saikal, 'Khomeini's Iran', *Current Affairs Bulletin*, 60:5 (October 1983), pp. 18–30.
6. For a critical assessment of the Islamic regime, see Martin Wright, *Iran: The Khomeini Revolution* (Harlow, Essex: Longman, 1989), esp. pp. 31–42; Hazhir Teimourian, 'Iran's 15 Years of Islam', *The World Today*, 50:4 (April 1994) 67–70; Darius M. Rejali, *Torture and Modernity: Self, Society, and State in Modern Iran* (Boulder: Westview Press, 1994), esp. chs 7–8.
7. For a detailed discussion, see Hamied Ansari, *Egypt: The Stalled Society* (New York: State University of New York Press, 1986), esp. chs 10–11; Robert Springborg, *Mubarak's Egypt: Fragmentation of the Political Order* (Boulder: Westview Press, 1989).

8. For a concise discussion, see Tareq Y. Ismael and Jacqueline S. Ismael *et al.*, *Politics and Government in the Middle East and North Africa* (Florida: Florida International University Press, 1991), ch. 13.

9. 'Elections in Egypt', *Human Rights Watch Backgrounder* (October 2000).

10. For background information, see John P. Entelis, *Algeria: The Revolution Institutionalised* (Boulder: Westview Press, 1986), esp. chs 3–7.

11. For a discussion of the crisis, see Paul Schemm, 'Algeria's Return to its Past: Can the FIS Break the Vicious Cycle of History?', *Middle East Insight*, XI:2 (January–February 1995), pp. 36–9.

12. United Nations Development Program, *Arab Human Development Report 2002* (New York: UNDP, 2002), p. 2.

13. Ibid., p. 3.

14. Ibid., p. 85.

15. Ibid., p. 9.

16. See Charles J. Adams, 'Mawdudi and the Islamic State', in John L. Esposito (ed.), *Voices of Resurgent Islam* (New York: Oxford University Press, 1983), ch. 5.

17. For diverse views, see Mir Zohari Husain, *Global Islamic Politics* (New York: HarperCollins College Publishers, 1995); John O. Voll, *Islam: Continuity and Change in the Modern World*, 2nd edn (New York: Syracuse University Press, 1994).

6   Conclusion: The Way Forward

1. Cited in Azzam S. Tamimi, *Rachid Ghannouchi: A Democrat Within Islamism* (New York: Oxford University Press, 2001), p. 179.

2. Riaz Hassan, *Faithlines: Muslim Conceptions of Islam and Society* (Karachi: Oxford University Press, 2002), pp. 223–4.

3. See Bernard Lewis, 'Inheriting a history of hatred', *International Herald Tribune*, 11 September 2002; Bernard Lewis, *What Went Wrong? Western Impact and Middle Eastern Response* (New York: Oxford University Press, 2002); Daniel Pipes, *Militant Islam Reaches America* (New York: W.W. Norton, 2002).

4. Jimmy Carter, 'The Troubling New Face of America', *International Herald Tribune*, 6 September 2002.

5. See Madeleine Albright, 'The Allies are Troubled by Bush's Policies', *International Herald Tribune*, 23 May 2002.

6. Najam Sethi, 'Nothing much to cheer about', *International Herald Tribune*, 18 October 2002.

7. Officially, Pakistan's annual defence budget for the fiscal year of 2001–02 was about US$3.2 bn, approximately 4.6 per cent of its Gross Domestic Product and around 29–30 per cent of the national budget. But these figures do not fully reflect reality. An undetermined amount of military expenditure is hidden elsewhere in the budget (for example, in spending on communications infrastructure). When this is taken into account, the defence budget for 2001–02 was estimated at 50–60 per cent of the national budget. The defence

budget is not transparent, and two items in the official budget – 'defence administration' and 'defence services' – represent all military expenditures. Given the lack of democratic procedures to verify the defence budgetary allocations, the military is in a position to give whatever figures it wants in the interest of 'national security'. See *Stockholm International Peace Research Institute (SIPRI), Military Expenditures Data, 2001–2002*; United States Department of State, *Annual Report on Military Expenditures, 1998* (Washington, DC: US Department of State, February 1999).

8. See William Maley, 'The Reconstruction of Afghanistan', in Ken Booth and Tim Dunne (eds), *Worlds in Collision: Terror and the Future of Global Order* (London: Palgrave Macmillan, 2002), pp. 184–93.

9. See Amin Saikal, 'Afghanistan After the Loya Jirga', *Survival*, 44:3 (Autumn 2002), pp. 47–56.

10. The Bush Administration's former envoy to Afghanistan, James Dobbins, writes: 'So far, American and European pledges of aid to Afghanistan remain modest by comparisons with other recent efforts in post-conflict nation-building. Kosovo, for example, has a population of about 2 million, while Afghanistan's is 23 million. But Kosovo received several times more American and European assistance per capita to recover from 23 weeks of conflict than Afghanistan has received to rebuild from 20 years of civil war ... American funding for reconstruction has been quite limited', 'Afghanistan's Faltering Reconstruction', *New York Times*, 12 September 2002.

11. 'Security in Afghanistan', Editorial, *Washington Post*, 9 September 2002.

Bibliography

Abbas, M. (1995) *Through Secret Channels: The Road to Oslo* (Reading: Garnet).

Aburish, S.K. (1995) *The Rise, Corruption and Coming Fall of The House of Saud* (London: Bloomsbury).

——(1998) *Arafat: From Defender to Dictator* (London: Bloomsbury).

Acharya, A. (1989) *U.S. Military Strategy in the Gulf* (London: Routledge).

Adams, C.J. (1983) 'Mawdudi and the Islamic State', in John L. Esposito (ed.), *Voices of Resurgent Islam* (New York: Oxford University Press).

Ahmed, A.S. (1992) *Postmodernism and Islam* (London: Routledge).

——(1993) *The Making of Modern Turkey* (London: Routledge).

——(1995) *Living Islam: From Samarkand to Stornoway* (Harmondsworth: Penguin).

Ajami, F. (1999) *The Dream Palace of the Arabs: A Generation's Odyssey* (New York: Vintage Books).

Akhavi, S. (1980) *Religion and Politics in Contemporary Iran: Clergy–State Relations in the Pahlavi Period* (Albany: State University of New York Press).

Alagappa, M. and Inoguchi, T. (eds) (1999) *International Security Management and the United Nations* (Tokyo: United Nations University Press).

Albright, M. (2002) 'The Allies are Troubled by Bush's Policies', *International Herald Tribune*, 23 May.

Ali, T. (2002) *The Clash of Fundamentalisms: Crusades, Jihads and Modernity* (London: Verso).

Al-Suwaidi, J.S. (ed.) (1996) *Iran and the Gulf: A Search for Stability* (Abu Dhabi: The Emirates Center for Strategic Studies and Research).

Ambrose, S.E. (1993) *Rise to Globalism: American Foreign Policy Since 1938* (Harmondsworth: Penguin).

Amuzegar, J. (1991) *The Dynamics of the Iranian Revolution: The Pahlavis' Triumph and Tragedy* (New York: State University of New York Press).

Ansari, H. (1986) *Egypt: The Stalled Society* (New York: State University of New York Press).

Arblaster, A. (1987) *Democracy* (Milton Keynes: Open University Press).

Arjomand, S.A. (1988) *The Turban for the Crown: The Islamic Revolution in Iran* (New York: Oxford University Press).

Armstrong, K. (2000) *Islam: A Short History* (New York: Modern Library).

Aronson, G. (1996) 'Settlement Monitor: Quarterly Update on Developments,' *Journal of Palestine Studies*, XXV:4 (Summer).

Avery, P. *et al.* (eds) (1991) *The Cambridge History of Iran*, Vol. 7 (Cambridge: Cambridge University Press).

Ayubi, N. (1991) *Political Islam: Religion and Politics in the Arab World* (London: Routledge).

Barber, B.R. (2001) *Jihad vs McWorld* (New York: Ballantine Books).

Beilin, Y. (1999) *Touching Peace: From the Oslo Accord to a Final Agreement* (trans. Philip Simpson) (London: Weidenfeld & Nicolson).

Benard, C. and Khalilzad, Z. (1984) *'The Government of God': Iran's Islamic Republic* (New York: Columbia University Press).

Bennis, P. (1997) *Clinton's Middle East Policy: Continuity or Change? Honest Broker? U.S. Policy and the Middle East Peace Process* (Washington, DC: The Center for Policy Analysis on Palestine, 1997).

Bill, J.A. (1988) *The Eagle and the Lion: The Tragedy of American–Iranian Relations* (New Haven: Yale University Press).

Bloodworth, D. (1975) *An Eye for The Dragon* (Harmondsworth: Penguin).

Bloom, J. and Blair, S. (2002) *Islam: A Thousand Years of Faith and Power* (New Haven: Yale University Press).

Bolt, A. (2002) 'Holy War of Words', *Herald-Sun*, 30 May.

——— (2002) 'Giving Thanks Where Due', *Herald-Sun*, 3 June.

Borer, D.A. (1999) *Superpowers Defeated: Vietnam and Afghanistan Compared* (London: Frank Cass).

Bowker, R. (1996) *Beyond Peace: The Search for Security in the Middle East* (Boulder: Lynne Rienner).

Bowman, S. (2002) *Weapons of Mass Destruction: The Terrorist Threat* (Washington, DC: Congressional Research Service, The Library of Congress).

Brzezinski, Z., Scowcroft, B. and Murphy, R. (1997) 'Differentiated Containment', *Foreign Affairs*, 76:3 (May–June), pp. 20–30.

——— (2002) 'Confronting Anti-American Grievances', *New York Times*, 1 September.

Bull, H. (1977) *The Anarchical Society: A Study of Order in World Politics* (Basingstoke, UK: Macmillan).

Burke, S.M. and Ziring, L. (2nd edn) (1990) *Pakistan's Foreign Policy: An Historical Analysis* (Karachi: Oxford University Press).

Burki, S.J. (1991) *Pakistan: The Continuing Search for Nationhood* (Boulder: Westview Press).

Burns, J.F. (1999) 'Former Hanging Judge of Iran', *New York Times*, 23 October.

Bush, G. (1991) 'Address Before a Joint Session of the Congress on the Cessation of the Persian Gulf Conflict – 6 March 1991', Public Papers of the Presidents of the United States – President George Bush (Washington, DC: Office of the Federal Register), vol. 1.

Bush, George W. (2001) 'Address to a Joint Session of Congress and the American People', *New York Times*, 20 September.

Butler, R. (2000) *Saddam Defiant: The Threat of Weapons of Mass Destruction and the Crisis of Global Security* (London: Orion Books).

Camilleri, J.A. (ed.) (2001) *Religion and Culture in Asia Pacific: Violence or Healing?* (Melbourne: Vista).

Carley, P. (1995) *Turkey's Role in the Middle East* (Washington, DC: United States Institute of Peace).

Carter, J. (1985) *The Blood of Abraham* (Boston: Houghton Mifflin).

——— (2002) 'The Troubling New Face of America', *International Herald Tribune*, 6 September.

Chomsky, N. (2001) *September 11* (Crows Nest, NSW: Allen & Unwin).

Chubin, S. and Zabiah, S. (1974) *The Foreign Relations of Iran: A Developing State in a Zone of Great-Power Conflict* (Berkeley: University of California Press).

Cleveland, W. (1985) *Islam Against the West* (London: Al-Saqi Books).

Congressional Record, 93:5, p. 6341, 80th Congress, 1st Session, 4 June 1947, House.

Congressional Record, Appendix, 93:12, p. 2968, 80th Congress, 1st Session, 19 June 1947, House.

Cooley, J.K. (1999) *Unholy Wars: Afghanistan, America and International Terrorism* (London: Pluto Press).

Curzon, Lord G.N. (1966) *Persia and the Persian Question*, vol. I, repr. (London: Frank Cass).

Danspeckgruber, W.F. with Tripp, C.R.H. (1996) *The Iraq Aggression Against Kuwait: Strategic Lessons and Implications for Europe* (Boulder: Westview Press).

——(ed.) (2002) *The Self-Determination of Peoples. Community, Nation, and State in an Interdependent World* (Boulder: Lynne Rienner).

Davis, J.M. (1999) *Between Jihad and Salaam: Profiles in Islam* (New York: St. Martin's).

de Tocqueville, A. (1956) *Democracy in America*, ed. and abr. by Richard D. Heffner (New York: Mentor).

DiGeorgio-Lutz, J.A. (1996) *The US–PLO Relationship: From Dialogue to the White House Lawn, the Middle East and the United States: A Historical and Political Reassessment* (Boulder: Westview Press).

Dion, R.R. (1999) *The Future of the Caspian: Prospects for the Region's Oil and Gas Industry* (London: The Petroleum Economist).

Donnan, H. (ed.) (2002) *Interpreting Islam* (London: Sage).

Dupree, L. (1980) *Afghanistan* (Princeton: Princeton University Press).

Dwyer, K. (1991) *Arab Voices: The Human Rights Debate in the Middle East* (London: Routledge and University of California Press).

Eickelman, D.F. and Piscatori, J. (1996) *Muslim Politics* (Princeton: Princeton University Press).

'Elections in Egypt' (2000) *Human Rights Watch Backgrounder* (October).

Entelis, J.P. (1986) *Algeria: The Revolution Institutionalised* (Boulder: Westview Press).

Esposito, J.L. (1992) *The Islamic Threat: Myth or Reality?* (New York: Oxford University Press).

——(ed.) (1995) *The Oxford Encyclopedia of the Modern Islamic World*, vols 1–4 (New York: Oxford University Press).

——(ed.) (1997) *Political Islam: Revolution, Radicalism or Reform?* (Boulder: Lynne Rienner).

——(2002) *Unholy War: Terror in the Name of Islam* (New York: Oxford University Press).

Falk, R. (1992) *Exploration at the Edge of Time: The Prospects for World Order* (Philadelphia: Temple University Press).

——(1995) *On Humane Governance: Toward a New Global Politics* (Pennsylvania: Pennsylvania State University Press).

———(1999) *Predatory Globalization* (Malden, MA: Polity Press).

Foreign Relations of the United States, Diplomatic Papers: The British Commonwealth, the Near East and Africa (1959) (Washington, DC: Government Printing Office).

Foundation for Middle East Peace (2001) 'Clinton's Departure, Intifada, and Israeli Elections Signal New Phase in Diplomacy', Report on Israeli Settlement in the Occupied Territories, 11:1.

Fromkin, D. (1991) *A Peace to End All Peace: Creating the Modern Middle East, 1914–1922* (Harmondsworth: Penguin).

Fry, G. and O'Hagan, J. (2000) *Contending Images of World Politics* (London: Macmillan).

Fuller, G. and Lesser, I.O. *et al.* (1993) *Turkey's New Geopolitics: From the Balkans to Western China* (Boulder: Westview Press).

Gaddis, J.L. (1987) *The Long Peace: Inquiries into the History of the Cold War* (Oxford: Oxford University Press).

Gause III, F.G. (2000) 'Saudi Arabia: Over a Barrel,' *Foreign Affairs,* 79:3 (May/June).

Gerges, F.A. (1994) *The Superpowers and the Middle East: Regional and International Politics, 1955–1967* (Boulder: Westview Press).

Gerner, D.J. (ed.) (2000) *Understanding the Contemporary Middle East* (Boulder: Lynne Rienner).

Ghobar, M.G.M. (2001) *Afghanistan in the Course of History,* Vol. 2 (trans. S.A. Fayez) (Herendon, VA: All Prints).

Gibb, H.A.R. (1975) *Islam: A Historical Survey* (Oxford: Oxford University Press).

Gill, K.P.S. and Ajai, S. (eds) (2002) *The Global Threat of Terror: Ideological, Material and Political Linkages* (New Delhi: Bulwark Books and Institute for Conflict Management).

Gilpin, R. (1981) *War and Change in World Politics* (Cambridge: Cambridge University Press).

Goldberg, J.J. (1996) *Jewish Power: Inside the American Jewish Establishment* (Reading: Addison-Wesley).

Goodwin, J. (1998) *Lords of the Horizons: A History of the Ottoman Empire* (New York: H. Holt).

Grare, F. (2001) *Political Islam in the Indian Subcontinent: The Jammat-I-Isalami* (New Delhi: Manohar Publishers).

Green, J.D. (1995) 'Gulf Security without the Gulf States?', *The Harvard Journal of World Affairs,* 4:1.

———(2000) *Leadership Succession in the Arab World* (Santa Monica: RAND).

Griffin, M. (2001) *Reaping the Whirlwind: The Taliban Movement in Afghanistan* (London: Pluto Press).

Guillanume, A. (1973) *Islam* (Harmondsworth: Penguin).

Gunaratna, R. (2002) *Inside Al Qaeda: Global Network of Terror* (London: Hurst).

Haddad, Y.Y. (1996) *Islamist Perceptions of US Policy in the Middle East. The Middle East and the United States: A Historical and Political Reassessment* (Boulder: Westview Press).

Hallaq, W.B. (1984) 'Was the Gate of *Ijtihad* Closed', *International Journal of Middle East Studies,* 16.

——— (1986) 'On the Origins of the Controversy about the existence of Mujtahids and the Gate of Ijtihad', *Studia Islamica*, 63, pp. 129–41.

Halliday, F. (1996) *Islam and the Myth of Confrontation: Religion and Politics in the Middle East* (London: I.B. Tauris).

Halsell, G. (1988) 'Israeli Extremists and Christian Fundamentalists: The Alliance', *Washington Report on Middle East Affairs*.

Hanks, R.J. (1980) *Oil and Security in U.S. Policy Towards the Arabian Gulf-Indian Ocean Area. Oil and Security in the Arab Gulf* (London: The Arab Research Centre).

Haqqani, H. (2002) 'Islam's Medieval Outposts', *Foreign Policy*, 133 (November–December).

Hassan, R. (2002) *Faithlines: Muslim Conceptions of Islam and Society* (Karachi: Oxford University Press).

Hayes, J.R. (ed.) (1983) *The Genius of Arab Civilization: Source of Renaissance* (London: Eurabia).

Heikal, M. (1986) *Cutting the Lion's Tail: Suez Through Egyptian Eyes* (London: Andre Deutsch)

——— (1992) *Illusions of Triumph: An Arab View of the Gulf War* (London: Harper Collins).

Held, D. (1992) 'Democracy: From City-states to a Cosmopolitan Order', *Political Studies*, XL: Special Issue, pp.10–39.

Henry, C.M. and Springborg, R. (2001) *Globalization and the Politics of Development in the Middle East* (Cambridge: Cambridge University Press).

Hermassi, E. (1972) *Leadership and National Development in North Africa: A Comparative Study* (Berkeley: University of California Press).

Hirst, D. (1984) *The Gun and the Olive Branch: The Roots of Violence in the Middle East* (London: Faber & Faber).

Hitti, P.K. (1970) *The Arabs: A Short History* (Washington, DC: Regnery Gateway).

Hoffman, S. (2000) *World Disorders: Troubled Peace in the Post-Cold War Era* (Lanham: Rowman & Littlefield).

Hollis, R. (2002) 'The U.S., Terrorism and the Middle East', *Asian Affairs*, XXXIII (February).

Holsti, O.R. and James, R.N. (1984) *American Leadership in World Affairs: Vietnam and the Breakdown of Consensus* (London: Allen & Unwin).

Hopkirk, P. (1992) *The Great Game: The Struggle for Empire in Central Asia* (New York: Kodansha International).

Hopwood, P. (1992) *Nasser* (London: Longman).

Hourani, A. (1991) *History of the Arab Peoples* (New York: Warner Books, 1991).

Huntington, S.P. (1998) *The Clash of Civilizations and the Remaking of World Order* (London: Touchstone Books).

——— (1999) 'The Lonely Superpower', *Foreign Affairs*, 78:2 (March/April).

Husain, M.Z. (1995) *Global Islamic Politics* (New York: HarperCollins College Publishers).

Indyk, M. (1993) *The Clinton Administration's Approach to the Middle East* (Washington, DC: Washington Institute for Near East Policy).

——— (2002) 'Back to the Bazaar' *Foreign Affairs*, 81:1.

Ismael, T.Y. and Ismael, J.S. *et al.* (1991) *Politics and Government in the Middle East and North Africa* (Florida: Florida International University Press).

Johnson, C. (2000) *Blowback: The Cost and Consequences of American Empire* (New York: An Owl Book).

Kandiyoti, D. (1996) *Gendering the Middle East: Emerging Perspectives* (London: I.B. Tauris).

Keddie, N.R. (1968) *An Islamic Response to Imperialism: Political and Religious Writings of Sayyid Jamal al-Din 'al-Afghani'* (Berkeley and Los Angeles: University of California Press).

Kemp, G. (1998–99) 'The Persian Gulf Remains the Strategic Prize', *Survival* 40:4 (Winter).

———— and Stein, J.G. (eds) (1995) *Powder Keg in the Middle East: The Struggle for Gulf Security* (Lanham: Rowman & Littlefield).

Kennedy, P. (1987) *The Rise and Fall of the Great Powers: Economic Change and Military Conflict from 1500 to 2000* (New York: Random House).

Kepel, G. (2002) *Jihad: The Trail of Political Islam* (trans. Anthony F. Roberts) (Cambridge, MA: Belknap Press of Harvard University Press).

Kerr, M.H. (1971) (3rd edn) *The Arab Cold War: Gamal Abd al-Nasser and his Rivals, 1858–1970* (Oxford: Oxford University Press).

Khalilzad, Z. and Byman, D. (2000) 'Afghanistan: The Consolidation of a Rogue State', *The Washington Quarterly*, 23:1.

Khatami, S.M. (1997) 'Statement made by President of the Islamic Republic of Iran and Chairman of the Eighth Session of the Islamic Summit Conference Tehran, 9 December 1997', *Iranian Journal of International Affairs*, IX:4 (Winter 1997/98) p. 601.

———— (1999) 'Dialogue and the New Millennium', Address delivered to the 30th General Conference of the United Nations Educational, Scientific and Cultural Organization (UNESCO), Paris, 29 October.

———— (2000) *Islam, Dialogue and Civil Society* (Canberra: Centre for Arab and Islamic Studies, Australian National University).

Khomeini, R. (1979) *Islamic Government* (New York: Manor).

Khomeini, R. (1990) *Sahifey-e Noor* (The Book of Light) vol. 21 (Tehran: Markaz-e Madarek Anghlab-e Islami).

Kissinger, H. (1994) *Diplomacy* (New York: Simon & Schuster).

———— (1999) *Years of Renewal: The Concluding Volume of His Memoirs* (New York: Simon & Schuster).

———— (2001) *Does America Need a Foreign Policy?: Toward a Diplomacy for the 21st Century* (New York: Simon & Schuster).

Kremmer, C. (2002) *The Carpet Wars* (Sydney: HarperCollins).

Kunihiolm, V.R. (1980) *The Origins of the Cold War in the Near East: Great Power Conflict and Diplomacy in Iran, Turkey and Greece* (Princeton: Princeton University Press).

Lamb, C. (1992) *Waiting for Allah: Benazir Bhutto and Pakistan* (Harmondsworth: Penguin).

Laqueur, W. (1972) *The Struggle for the Middle East: The Soviet Union and the Middle East 1958–68* (Harmondsworth: Penguin).

Lebow, R.N. and Stein, J.G. (1994) *We All Lost the Cold War* (Princeton: Princeton University Press).

Lenczowski, G. (1949) *Russia and the West in Iran, 1918–1948: A Study in Big-Power Rivalry* (Ithaca: Cornell University Press).

Lesch, A.M. and Tessler, M. (1989) *Israel, Egypt, and Palestinians: From Camp David to Intifada* (Bloomington: Indiana University Press).

Lesch, D. (ed.) (1999) (2nd edn) *The Middle East and the United States: A Historical and Political Reassessment* (Boulder: Westview Press).

Lewis, B. (1988) *The Political Language of Islam* (Chicago: University of Chicago Press).

——— (1993) *Islam and the West* (New York: Oxford University Press).

——— (1996) *The Middle East: 2000 Years of History From the Rise of Christianity to the Present Day* (London: Phoenix).

——— (2002) 'Inheriting a history of hatred', *International Herald Tribune*, 11 September.

——— (2002) *What Went Wrong? Western Impact and Middle Eastern Response* (New York: Oxford University Press).

Low, D.A. (ed.) (1991) *The Political Inheritance of Pakistan* (London: Macmillan).

McCauley, M. (2002) *Afghanistan and Central Asia: A Modern History* (London: Longman).

McChesney, R.D. (1996) *Central Asia: Foundations of Change* (Princeton: Darwin Press).

Mackenzie, R. (1998) 'The United States and the Taliban', in William Maley (ed.), *Fundamentalism Reborn? Afghanistan and the Taliban* (London: Hurst).

Mackey, S. (1996) *The Iranians: Persia, Islam and the Soul of a Nation* (New York: Dutton).

Makiya, K. (1994) *Cruelty and Silence: War, Tyranny, Uprising and the Arab World* (Harmondsworth: Penguin).

Maley, W. (1998) 'Interpreting the Taliban', in William Maley (ed.), *Fundamentalism Reborn? Afghanistan and the Taliban* (London: Hurst).

——— (2000) *The Foreign Policy of the Taliban* (New York: Council on Foreign Relations).

——— (2002) 'The Reconstruction of Afghanistan', in Ken Booth and Tim Dunne (eds), *Worlds in Collision: Terror and the Future of Global Order* (London: Palgrave Macmillan).

——— (2002) *The Afghanistan Wars* (London: Palgrave Macmillan).

Mansfield, P. (1991) *A History of the Middle East* (Harmondsworth: Penguin).

Mansour, C. (1994) *Beyond Alliance: Israel in US Foreign Policy* (New York: Columbia University Press).

——— (2001) 'The Oslo Breakdown: Israel's Colonial Impasse', *Journal of Palestine Studies*, 30:4 (Summer).

Mark, C.R. (2002) 'Israel: US Foreign Assistance', *Issue Brief for Congress* (Washington, DC: Congressional Research Service, 6 June).

Mead, W.R. (1999/2000) 'The Jacksonian Tradition and American Foreign Policy' *The National Interest*, 58 (Winter)

Melman, Y. and Raviv, D. (1994) *Friends in Deed: Inside the US–Israel Alliance* (New York: Hyperion).

Mernissi, F. (1993) *Islam and Democracy: Fear of the Modern World* (trans. M.J. Lakeland) (London: Virago Press).

Milani, M.M. (1994) (2nd edn) *The Making of Iran's Islamic Revolution: From Monarchy to Islamic Republic* (Boulder: Westview Press).

The Military Balance, 1994–1995 (1995) (London: International Institute for Strategic Studies).

Miller, A. (1980) *Search for Security: Saudi Arabian Oil and American Foreign Policy, 1939–1949* (Chapel Hill: University of North Carolina Press).

Mojtahed-Zadeh, P. (2001) 'The Caspian Sea Regime: A Geographical Perspective of an Obstacle in the Way of Regional Cooperation', *The Iranian Journal of International Affairs*, XIII:1 (Spring).

——— (2001) 'Geopolitics and Reform Under Khatami', *Global Dialogue*, 3:2–3 (Summer).

Mortimer, E. (1982) *Faith and Power: The Politics of Islam* (London: Faber & Faber).

Mottahedeh, R.P. (1980) *Loyalty and Leadership in an Early Islamic Society*, (Princeton: Princeton University Press).

——— (1986) *The Mantle of the Prophet: Learning and Power in Modern Iran* (London: Chatto & Windus).

Nye Jr, J.S. (1990) *Bound to Lead: The Changing Nature of American Power* (New York: Basic Books).

——— (2002) *The Paradox of American Power: Why the World's Only Superpower Can't Go it Alone* (New York: Oxford University Press).

——— and Donahue, J.D. (eds) (2000) *Governance in a Globalizing World* (Washington, DC: Brookings Institution Press).

Parsons, A. (1995) *From Cold War to Hot Peace: UN Interventions, 1947–1994* (London: Michael Joseph).

Peters, R. (trans.) (1977) *Jihad in Medieval and Modern Islam: The Chapter on Jihad from Averroes' Legal Handbook 'Bidayat al-mudjtahid' and the Treatise 'Koran and Fighting' by the Late Shaykh-al-Azhar, Mahmud Shaltut* (Leiden: Brill).

Phillips, J. (2001) *Building Bridges on Sand: Clinton's Dubious Middle East Peace Initiative* (Washington, DC: Heritage Foundation).

Pipes, D. (2002) *Militant Islam Reaches America* (New York: W.W. Norton).

Piscatori, J.P. (1986) *Islam in a World of Nation-States* (Cambridge: Cambridge University Press).

——— (ed.) (1991) *Islamic Fundamentalisms and the Gulf Crisis* (New York: American Academy of Arts and Sciences).

Quandt, W.B. (rev. edn) (2001) *Peace Process: American Diplomacy and the Arab–Israeli Conflict Since 1967* (Washington, DC: Brookings Institution Press and University of California Press).

Ramazani, R.K. (1975) *Iran's Foreign Policy, 1941–1973: A Study of Foreign Policy in Modernising Nations* (Charlottesville: University Press of Virginia).

Rashid, A. (1998) 'Pakistan and the Taliban', in William Maley (ed.), *Fundamentalism Reborn? Afghanistan and the Taliban* (London: Hurst).

——— (2000) *Taliban: Militant Islam, Oil and Fundamentalism in Central Asia* (New Haven: Yale Nota Bene, Yale University Press).

Rejali, D.M. (1994) *Torture and Modernity: Self, Society, and State in Modern Iran* (Boulder: Westview Press).

Reuveny, R. and Parkash, A. (1999) 'The Afghanistan War and the Breakdown of the Soviet Union', *Review of International Studies*, 25:4, pp. 693–708.

Robinson, G.E. (1997) *Building a Palestinian State: The Incomplete Revolution* (Bloomington: Indiana University Press).

Rouleau, E. (2002) 'Trouble in the Kingdom', *Foreign Affairs*, 81:4 (July–August).

Roy, O. (1990) *Islam and Resistance in Afghanistan* (Cambridge: Cambridge University Press).

——(1994) *The Failure of Political Islam* (Cambridge, MA: Harvard University Press).

——(1995) *Afghanistan: From Holy War to Civil War* (Princeton: Darwin Press).

——(2000) *The New Central Asia: The Creation of Nations* (New York: New York University Press).

Rubin, B. (1993) 'The United States and Iraq: From Appeasement to War', in Amatzia Baram and Barry Rubin (eds), *Iraq's Road to War* (London: Macmillan).

——(1995) *The Fragmentation of Afghanistan: State Formation and Collapse in the International System* (New Haven: Yale University Press).

——(1995) *The Search for Peace in Afghanistan: From Buffer State to Failed State* (New Haven: Yale University Press).

——(1999) *The Transformation of Palestinian Politics: From Revolution to State-building* (Cambridge, MA: Harvard University Press).

Rustow, D.A. and Mugno, J.F. (1976) *OPEC: Success and Prospects* (New York: New York University Press).

——(1992) *Oil and Turmoil: America Faces OPEC and the Middle East* (New York: W.W. Norton).

Ruthveb, M. (1985) *Islam in the World* (Harmondsworth: Penguin).

Sachedina, A. (2001) *The Islamic Roots of Democratic Pluralism* (New York: Oxford University Press).

Safan, N. (1985) *Saudi Arabia: The Ceaseless Quest for Security* (Cambridge, MA: Harvard University Press).

Said, E.W. (1979) *Orientalism* (New York: Vintage Books).

——(1992) *The Question of Palestine* (London: Vintage).

——(1993) *Culture and Imperialism* (London: Chatto & Windus).

——(1997) *Covering Islam* (New York: Vintage Books).

——(2001) (rev. edn), *The End of the Peace Process: Oslo and After* (New York: Random House).

——(2001) 'Two Civilisations, Deeply Entwined', *The Age*, 23 October.

Saikal, A. (1980) *The Rise and Fall of the Shah* (Princeton: Princeton University Press).

——(1982–83) 'Kemalism: Its Influences on Iran and Afghanistan', *International Journal of Turkish Studies*, 2:2.

——(1983) 'Khomeini's Iran', *Current Affairs Bulletin*, 60:5. (October).

——(1985) 'Soviet Policy Toward Southwest Asia', *The Annals of the American Academy of Political and Social Science*, 481 (September).

——(1991) 'Iran's Foreign Policy 1921–1979', *Cambridge History of Iran*, vol. VII (Cambridge: Cambridge University Press).

——(1993) 'The New Face of the Middle East', *Ditchley Foundation Paper*, no. D92/14.

——(1993) 'The West and Post-Khomeini Iran', *The World Today*, 49:10.

————(1994) 'Regional Politics After the Gulf War', in Hubert Blumberg and Christopher French (eds), *The Persian Gulf War: Views from the Social and Behavioral Sciences* (Lanham, Maryland: University Press of America).

————(1995) 'Russia and Central Asia', in Amin Saikal and William Maley (eds), *Russia in Search of its Future* (Cambridge: Cambridge University Press).

————(1996) 'The American Approach to the Security of the Gulf', in Wolfgang F. Danspeckgruber and Charles R.H. Tripp (eds), *The Iraqi Aggression Against Kuwait: Strategic Lessons and Implications for Europe* (Boulder: Westview Press).

————(1996) 'The UN and Afghanistan: A Case of Failed Peacemaking Intervention?' *International Peacekeeping*, 3:1 (Spring).

————(1998) 'Afghanistan's Ethnic Conflict', *Survival*, 40:2 (Summer).

————(1998) 'The Role of the United Nations in the Middle East', in Tom Woodhouse, Robert Bruce and Malcolm Dando (eds), *Peacekeeping and Peacemaking: Towards Effective Intervention in Post-Cold War Conflict* (New York: St Martin's Press).

————(1999) 'Regional Conflicts and Cross-Border Ethnonationalism in Southwest Asia', in Majid Tehranian (ed.), *Asian Peace: Security and Governance in the Asia–Pacific Region* (London: I.B. Tauris).

————(2000) 'Dimensions of State Disruption and International Responses', *Third World Quarterly*, 21:1.

————(2000) 'The Role of Outside Actors in Afghanistan', *Middle East Policy*, VII:4.

————(2002) 'Afghanistan After the Loya Jirga', *Survival*, 44:3 (Autumn).

————(2002) 'The Coercive Disarmament of Iraq', in Susan Wright (ed.), *Biological Warfare and Disarmament: New Problems/New Perspectives* (New York: Rowman-Littlefield)

————and William Maley (1991) *Regime Change in Afghanistan: Foreign Intervention and the Politics of Legitimacy* (Boulder: Westview Press).

Sajjadpour, S.M.K. (1995) 'The Policy of Dual Containment in Theory and Practice', *The Iranian Journal of International Affairs*, VII:1.

Satloff, R. (2002) 'The Karine-A Affair and the War on Terrorism', *The National Interest*, 67 (Spring).

Schacht, J. (1975) *The Origins of Muhammadan Jurisprudence* (Oxford: Clarendon Press).

Schacht, J. and Bosworth, C.E. (1979) (2nd edn) *The Legacy of Islam* (Oxford: Oxford University Press).

Schemm, P. (1995) 'Algeria's Return to its Past: Can the FIS Break the Vicious Cycle of History?', *Middle East Insight*, XI:2 (January–February), pp. 36–9.

Schiff, Z. and Ya'ari, E. (1990) *Intifada: The Palestinian Uprising – Israel's Third Front* (trans. Ina Freedman) (New York: Simon & Schuster).

Schultz, G.P. (1993) *Turmoil and Triumph: Diplomacy, Power, and the Victory of the American Ideal* (New York: Charles Scribner).

Sciolino, E. (2000) *Persian Mirrors: The Elusive Face of Iran* (New York: The Free Press).

Sethi, N. (2002) 'Nothing much to cheer about', *International Herald Tribune*, 18 October.

Shlaim, A. (2000) *The Iron Wall: Israel and the Arab World* (Harmondsworth: Penguin).

Sick, G. (1985) *All Fall Down: America's Fateful Encounter with Iran* (London: I.B. Tauris).

Siftry, M.L. and Cerf, C. (eds) (1991) *The Gulf War Reader: History, Documents, Opinion* (New York: Random House).

Smith, W.C. (1957) *Islam in Modern History* (New York: Mentor).

Springborg, R. (1989) *Mubarak's Egypt: Fragmentation of the Political Order* (Boulder: Westview Press).

Sprout, H. and Sprout, M. (1946) *The Rise of American Naval Power, 1776–1918* (Princeton: Princeton University Press).

Statistical Yearbook 1993 (1995) (New York: United Nations).

Steinberg, D.J. *et al.* (1971) *In Search of Southeast Asia* (London: Pall Mall Press).

Stockholm International Peace Research Institute (SIPRI), Military Expenditures Data, 2001–2002.

Stump, R.W. (2000) *Boundaries of Faith: Geographical Perspectives on Religious Fundamentalism* (Lanham: Rowman & Littlefield).

Sullivan, D.J. and Abed-Kotob, S. (1999) *Islam in Contemporary Egypt: Civil Society vs the State* (Boulder: Lynne Rienner).

Tamimi, A.S. (2001) *Rachid Ghannouchi: A Democrat Within Islamism* (New York: Oxford University Press).

Teimourian, H. (1994) 'Iran's 15 Years of Islam', *The World Today*, 50:4 (April).

Theobald, A.B. (1951) *The Mahdiya: A History of the Anglo-Egyptian Sudan, 1881–1899* (London: Longmans Green).

United Nations Development Program (2002) *Arab Human Development Report 2002* (New York: UNDP).

United Nations Security Council, S/RES/1397 (12 March 2002).

United States Department of State (1951) *US State Department Bulletin*, 14:621 (28 May).

———(1953) *US State Department Bulletin*, 28 (9 February).

———(1999) *Annual Report on Military Expenditures, 1998* (Washington, DC: US Department of State, February).

Vakili, V. (1996) *Debating Religion and Politics in Iran: The Political Thought of Abdulkarim Soroush*, Occasional Paper Series no. 2 (New York: Council on Foreign Relations).

Voll, J.O. (1994) (2nd edn) *Islam: Continuity and Change in the Modern World* (New York: Syracuse University Press).

Walzer, M. (1992) *Just and Unjust Wars: A Moral Argument with Historical Illustrations* (New York: Basic Books).

Washington Report on Middle East Affairs, August/September 1996.

Waterbury, J. (1983) *The Egypt of Nasser and Sadat: The Political Economy of Two Regimes* (Princeton: Princeton University Press).

Watt, W.M. (1968) *What is Islam?* (New York: Praeger).

Weiss, B.G. (1978) 'Interpretation in Islamic Law: The Theory of *Ijtihad*', *American Journal of Comparative Law*, 26 (Spring) 199–212.

Wright, M. (1989) *Iran: The Khomeini Revolution* (Harlow, Essex: Longman).

Wright, R. (1986) *Sacred Rage: The Wrath of Militant Islam* (London: Andre Deutsch).

——— (1989) *In the Name of God: The Khomeini Decade* (New York: Simon & Schuster).

Yapp, M.E. (1991) *The Making of the Modern Near East 1792–1923* (London: Longman).

Zonis, M. (1991) *Majestic Failure: The Fall of the Shah* (Chicago: University of Chicago Press).

Zurcher, E.J. (1994) *Turkey: A Modern History* (London: I.B. Tauris).

Index